VINTAGE
FRENCH
NEEDLEWORK

Véronique Maillard

VINTAGE FRENCH NEEDLEWORK

300 Authentic Cross Stitch Patterns

Flowers, Borders, and Alphabets from Antique Textiles

SCHIFFER CRAFT

4880 Lower Valley Road • Atglen, PA 19310

Photo credits: Pierre Ferbos, pages 6, 238, 259, 314, 319, 328, 333, 347, 358, 370, 382, 384, 388, 395, 396, 398, 400, 403.
Frédéric Morellec, pages 12, 20, 24, 26, 33, 38, 60, 69, 78, 82–83, 103, 107, 110, 115.
Michel Azouz, page 374.
Émilie Verdier, pages 48, 166, 175, 202, 366, 376, 444–445.

Designed by Delphine Delastre
Type set in Penshurst Shadow/Gill Sans LT

ISBN: 978-0-7643-6764-9
Printed in China
5 4 3 2

Published by Schiffer Craft
An imprint of Schiffer Publishing, Ltd.
4880 Lower Valley Road
Atglen, PA 19310
Phone: (610) 593-1777; Fax: (610) 593-2002
Email: Info@schifferbooks.com
Web: www.schifferbooks.com

For our complete selection of fine books on this and related subjects, please visit our website at www.schifferbooks.com. You may also write for a free catalog.

Schiffer Publishing's titles are available at special discounts for bulk purchases for sales promotions or premiums. Special editions, including personalized covers, corporate imprints, and excerpts, can be created in large quantities for special needs. For more information, contact the publisher.

We are always looking for people to write books on new and related subjects. If you have an idea for a book, please contact us at proposals@schifferbooks.com.

CONTENTS

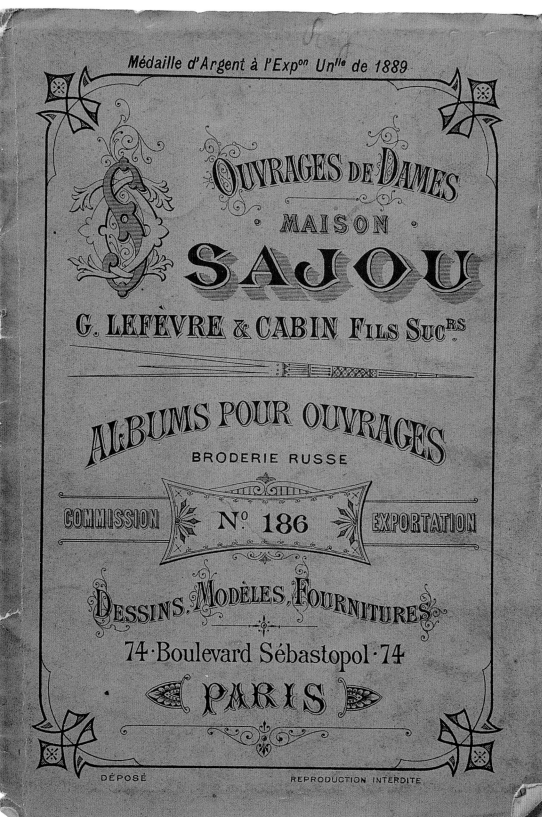

Médaille d'Argent à l'Exp^{on} Un^{lle} de 1889

OUVRAGES DE DAMES

MAISON

SAJOU

G. LEFÈVRE & CABIN FILS SUC^{RS}

ALBUMS POUR OUVRAGES

BRODERIE RUSSE

COMMISSION · N° 186 · EXPORTATION

DESSINS, MODÈLES, FOURNITURES

74 · Boulevard Sébastopol · 74

PARIS

DÉPOSÉ   REPRODUCTION INTERDITE

INTRODUCTION

Cross-stitch embroidery is part of our cultural heritage, and although it was not that long ago that people traditionally monogrammed their household linens (tablecloths, napkins, sheets, and the like), as well as some clothing, the cross-stitch pattern collections our foremothers used for that daily task are now a real rarity.

Like many of you, I am passionate about cross-stitch embroidery and am always on the lookout for new designs to adorn my pieces. A couple of years ago, when I wanted to personalize a gift for a friend, a neighbor gave me several illustrated booklets full of embroidery alphabets, old books she had been keeping since she was young. Later on, knowing I was interested in cross-stitching, a friend of my great-grandmother's entrusted me with a few more small illustrated books similar to them: cross-stitch pattern books that were published by the needlework and haberdashery firms of generations ago as a way to provide ladies with elegant patterns and ideas for their everyday work.

And that's how my collection was born. I have continued to search for these little booklets, or "mark manuals," which our ancestors used to prepare their dowry chests or to customize their household linens. Most of these alphabets were meant to be embroidered using cross stitching, but some of the mark manuals also featured whitework, bourdon embroidery, tatting, or crocheting.

The wealth of patterns to choose from is a genuine goldmine for passionate stitchers: in this book, you'll discover letters in all shapes, sizes, and styles (English, Gothic, floral, ornate, etc.), which can be adapted to any piece. Discovering the breadth of these, and continuing to embroider them, is the best way to save the needlecrafts of yesteryear.

Vintage alphabets can be applied to various projects: tablecloths and napkins, bath towels, clothing (aprons, blouses, etc.), and decorative objects like cushions, curtains, and sewing boxes.

There is no risk of you running out of ideas, as the photographs throughout these pages show. Up until not so many decades ago, monogramming linens was a pastime for the winter months for women of all ages. Each piece of table linen or household linen in a family home would feature the initials of their owner. When these initials are small, they are called "marks"; when they are large and ornate, they become "monograms."

FABRICS, EMBROIDERY FLOSS, AND NEEDLES

Although I have a personal preference for fine linen, decorative borders and alphabets can be embroidered on any type of fabric: muslin, aida fabric, old household linens of any cloth, or silk gauze. One thing is for certain: the finer the fabric, the smaller the stitches, and the more delicate and elegant the result.

Some of the borders and alphabets presented here are designed for two-tone embroidery, but it is of course up to you to interpret the designs according to your taste and imagination—or, to put it more simply, according to the application and use of your chosen project.

I generally use two types of embroidery floss:

• Mouliné Spécial DMC six-stranded floss (depending on the fabric and letters, I embroider using 1 or 2 strands), with a silky-smooth finish. There is a broad range of colors available.

The great advantage of this floss is that it is colorfast, which means that you can wash your pieces (even with a drop of bleach if necessary) without having to worry that the colors may fade. This is important when embroidering dish towels or napkins, and generally pieces that tend to get put in a washing machine relatively often.

• Soie d'Alger seven-stranded silk floss from Au Ver à Soie. Depending on the fabric and letters, I embroider using 1 or 2 strands of glossy floss. The range features about 700 colors with very subtle gradations in shades. This thread is better suited for embroidering decorative objects.

I use standard embroidery needles in different sizes, with blunt-ended tips. Of course, the more delicate the fabric the finer the needle you'll use, to avoid leaving holes. Only ever work with flawless needles that are not bent or rusted, to avoid damaging your work.

To make it easier for you, and to increase legibility, I have digitally transcribed the patterns gathered in this volume. As the title suggests, all patterns included in this book are designed for cross-stitch embroidery, either over one or two warp or weft threads. In the grids, each filled-in little square represents one cross stich. The presentation on a grid pattern corresponds exactly to that used in the old catalogs, including some irregularities (for example, individual letters that are oddly taller than the rest of the alphabet). Furthermore, watch out when embroidering floral alphabets: you may initially think that the same flower is used throughout, but if you look closely, you will notice that there are minuscule changes from one letter to the next. Don't be surprised either when these alphabets don't contain twenty-six letters: the I and the J are often conflated into one letter, and the W is formed of a V with an additional foot!

DESIGN PLACEMENT

It's always a good idea to properly center your work. Fold your fabric in four to find the middle, and mark it with basting stitches. Determine the center of your pattern on the grid. Counting the stitches will make it easier to judge how much space your design will take up before making a start. It is always aggravating to realize too late that you have run out of space to embroider an entire motif—which will happen to every single embroiderer at some point!

To ensure that your piece looks perfect both on the front and at the back (embroiderers traditionally got judged on their work based on the look of the reverse side!), never tie a knot at the end of the thread when you start. Begin by passing the floss through to the wrong side, then catch it with your first cross stitches.

When you have completed your work, you can cut off the remaining short ends to achieve a neat finish. At the end of your work, slip the last inches of thread through some stitches at the back to stop them from fraying when washing the piece.

Take care to always iron your work from the wrong side, to avoid flattening the floss.

You are holding in your hands an embroiderers' bible. The traditional look of this book beautifully reproduces the style of the first illustrated mark manuals and similar pattern books of the nineteenth century.

I wish you as much joy when embroidering these decorative borders, flowers, and alphabets as I had when restoring and compiling them for you. It's your turn now to choose your next letters, borders, or alphabets from these 300 grids to decorate your works. You will see, just as your foremothers did: their grace and elegance will embellish your homes and brighten up your days.

Old linen dish towel, personalized with different alphabets: "E" and "G" from the A. Rouyer alphabet, n° 249, "A" and "D" from the Sajou alphabet, n° 203, and "E" and "D" from A. Rouyer, n° 248.

A little multi-use bag, embroidered with two strands of Mouliné Spécial DMC six-stranded floss using the N. Alexandre alphabet, n° 229.

To make a cover for a recipe book, I embroidered an old dish towel using two strands of Mouliné Spécial DMC six-stranded floss: the top border is taken from the Sajou alphabet, n° 2, the capital letters "L" and "M" from Sajou, n° 605, and the other letters are Sajou, n° 3.

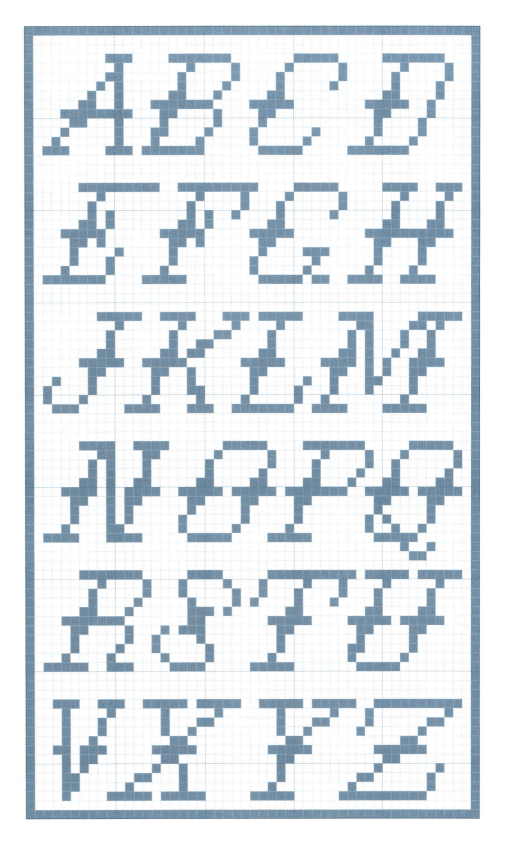

Sajou, n° 3 (letter height: 11 stitches)

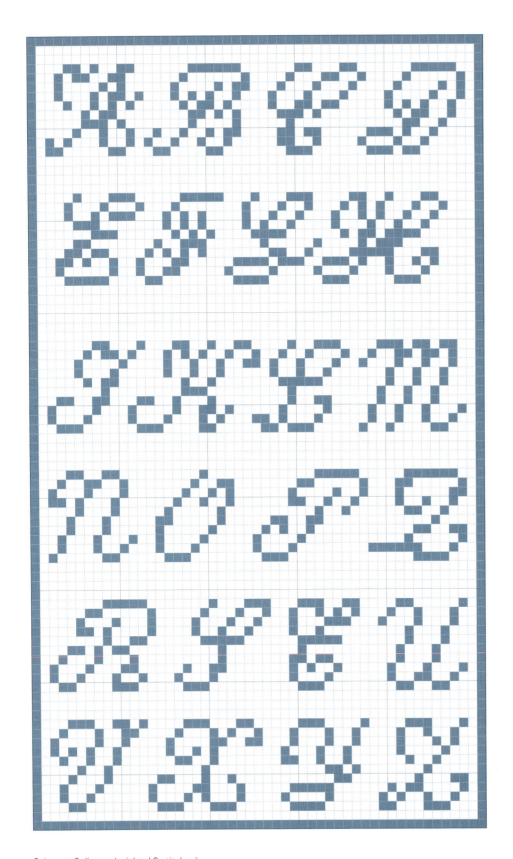

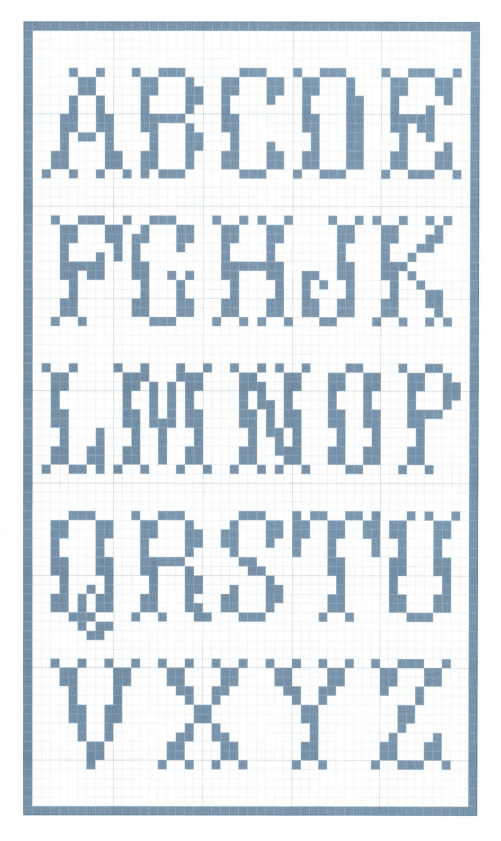

Sajou, n° 3 (letter height: 12 stitches)

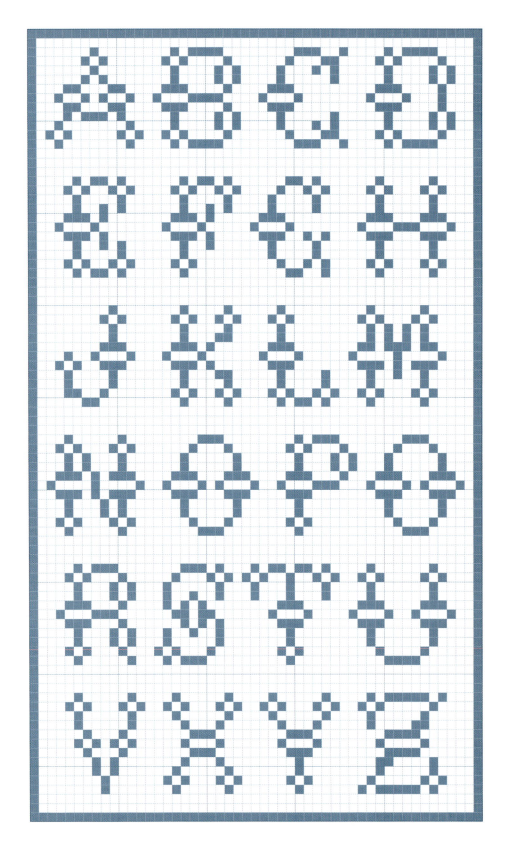

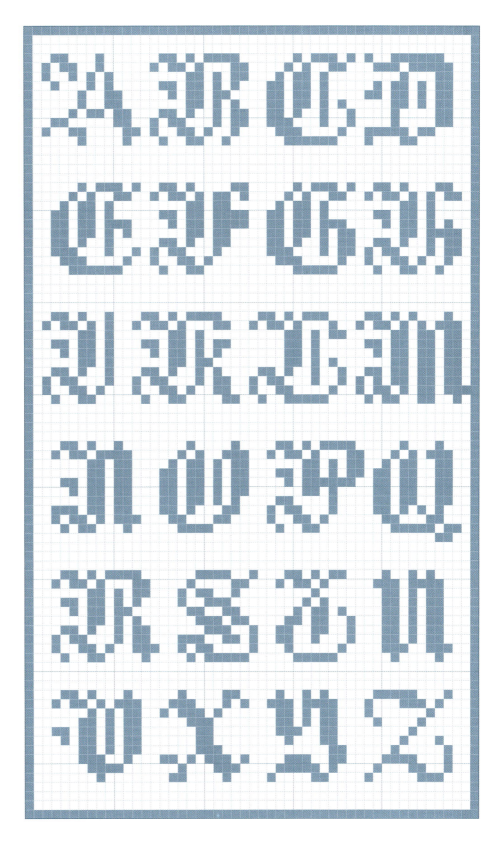

Sajou, n° 3 (letter height: 10 stitches)

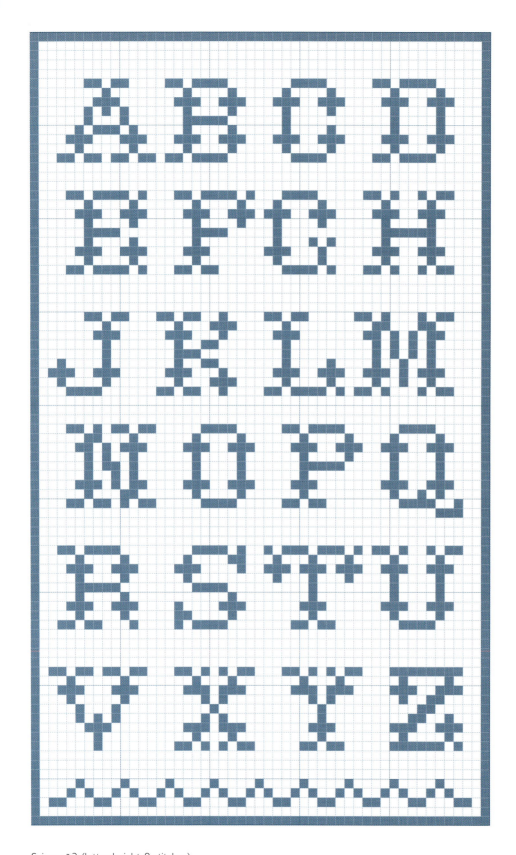

Sajou, n° 3 (letter height: 9 stitches)

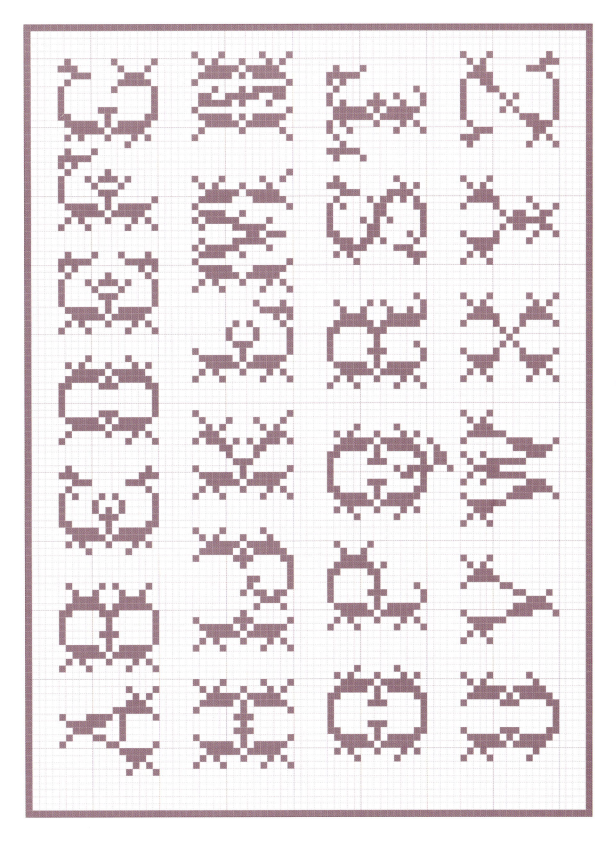

Sajou, n° 7 (letter height: 15 stitches)

While the baby naps . . . make the most of it and embroider
a bib with letters of the alphabet; Sajou, n° 52.

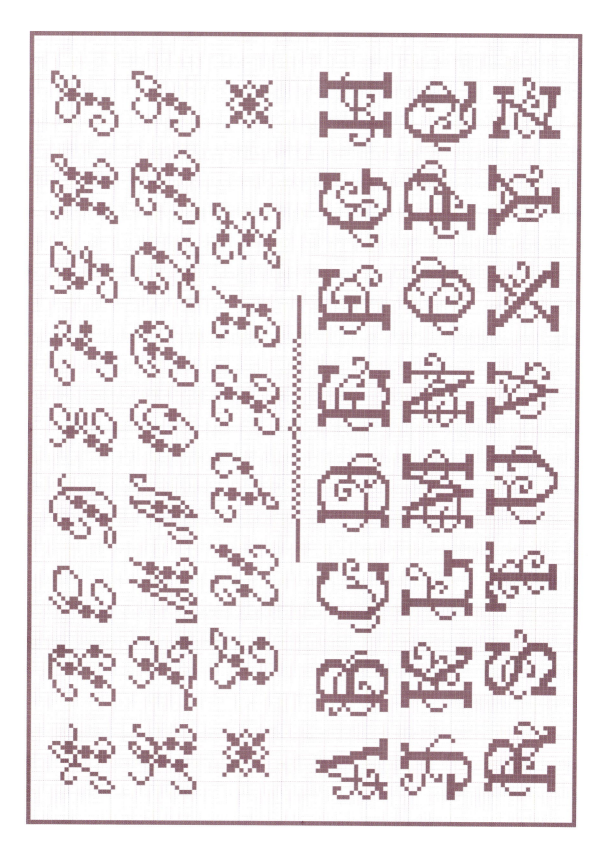

Sajou, n° 52 (letter height: first alphabet, 16 stitches; second alphabet, 17 stitches)

N. Alexandre, n° 211 (letter height: first alphabet, 5 stitches; second alphabet, 7 stitches; third alphabet, 9 stitches)

The first name *Baptiste*, using the A. Rouyer alphabet, n° 249, embroidered onto aida band that was then sewn onto a bath towel.

A little lavender bag made of embroidered aida band to be hung from the bathroom window, using letters from the Sajou alphabet, n° 2.

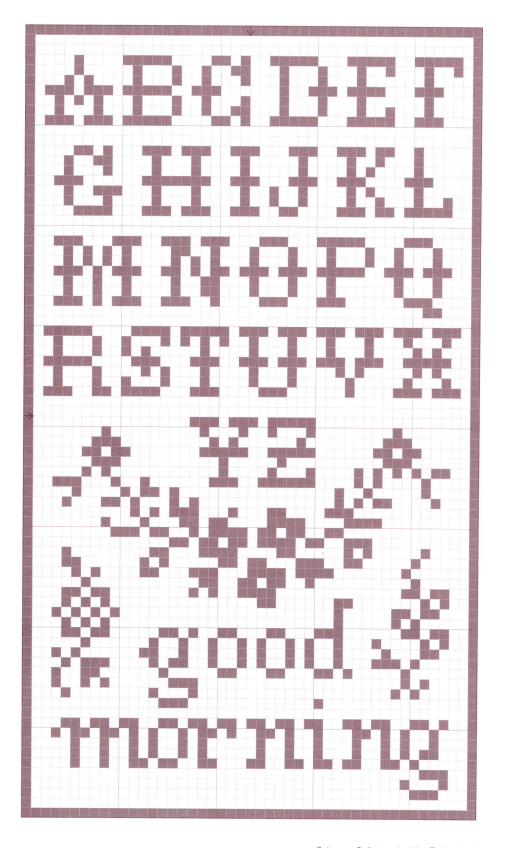

Sajou, n° 2 (letter height: 7 stitches)

Sajou, n° 103 (letter height: 7 stitches)

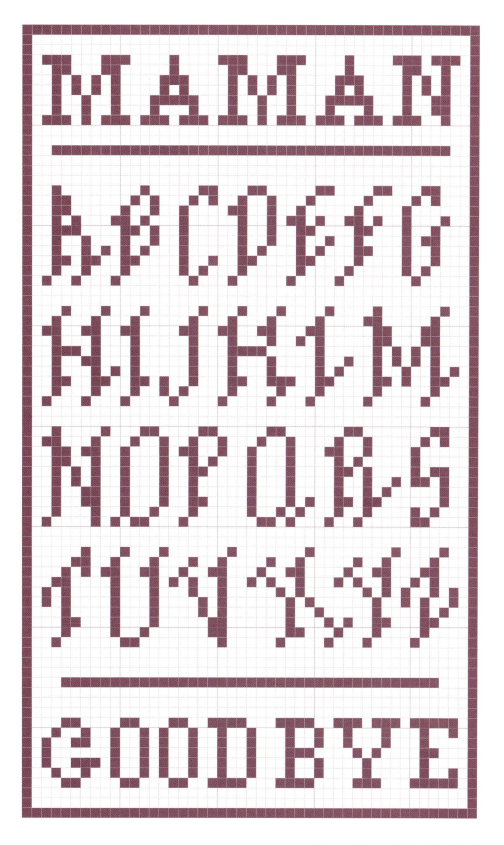

Sajou, n° 2 (letter height: 10 stitches)

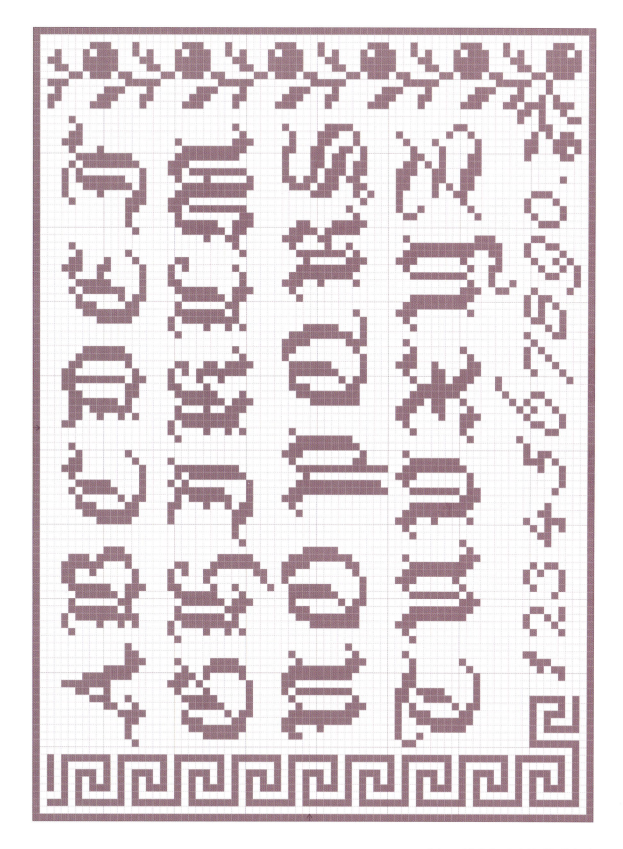

Sajou, n° 2 (letter height: 12 stitches)

A. Rouyer (from the World's Fair at The Hague, 1867–1868; letter height: 15 stitches)

Sajou, n° 103 (letter height: 10 stitches)

Sajou, n° 103 (letter height: 10 stitches)

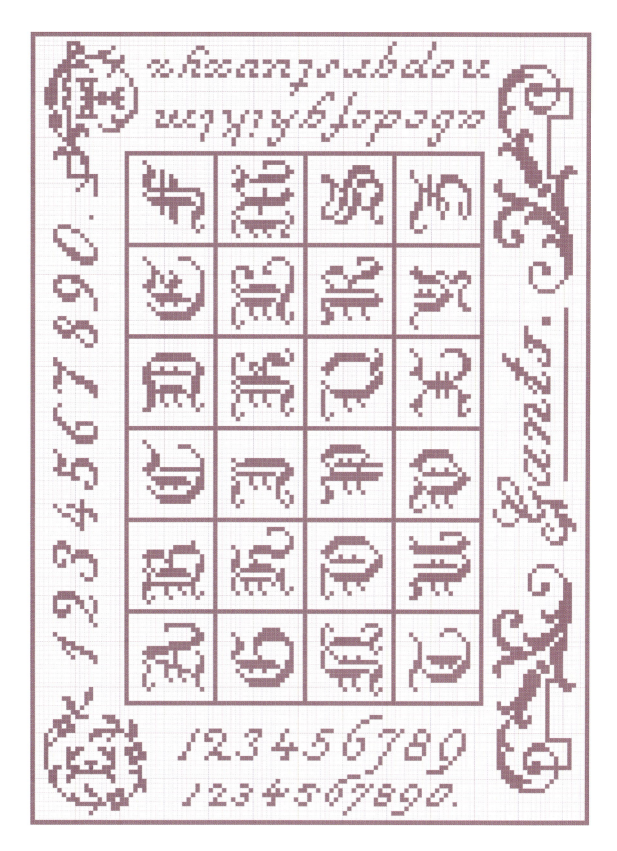

Sajou, n° 149 (letter height: 14 and 4 stitches)

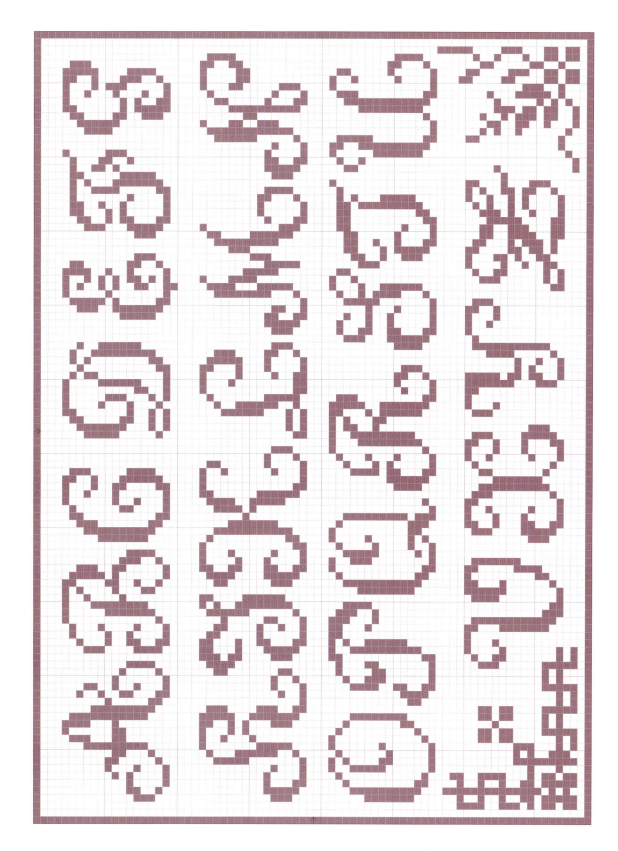

Sajou, n° 2 (letter height: 15 stitches)

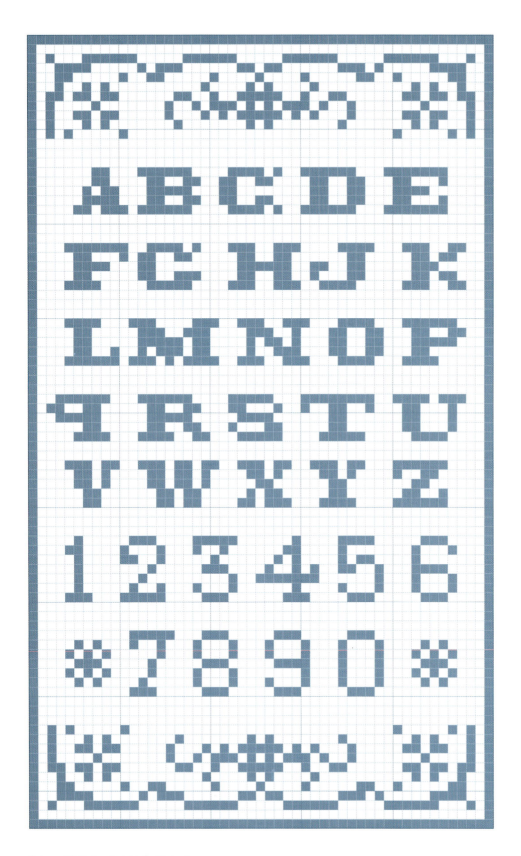

Sajou, n° 3 (letter height: 5 stitches)

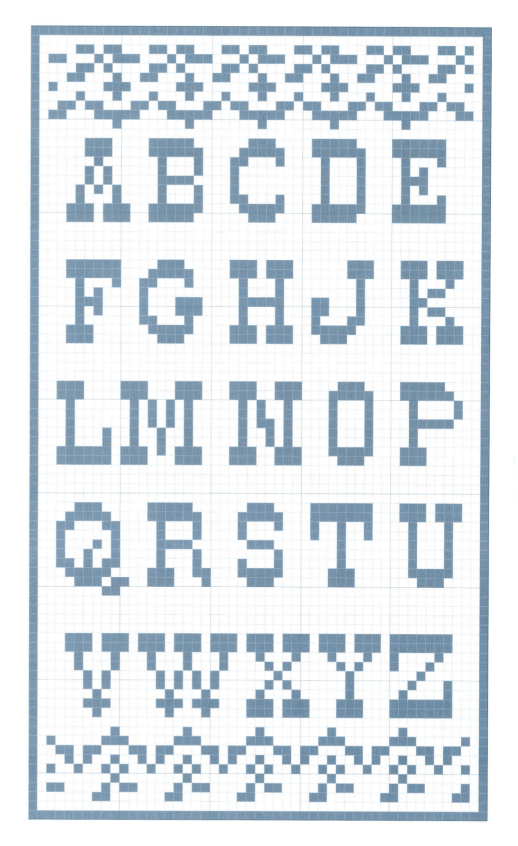

Sajou, n° 7 (letter height: 9 stitches)

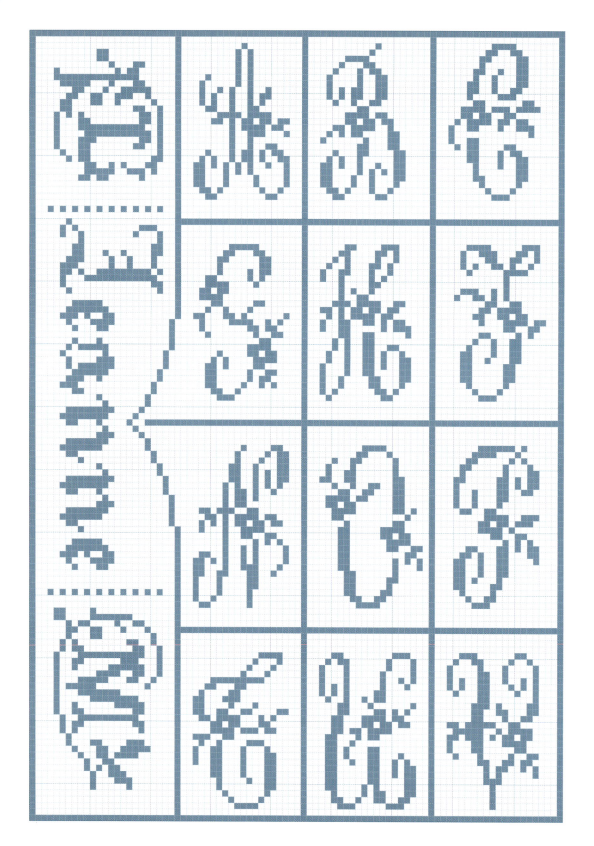

Sajou, n° 149 (letter height: 25 stitches)

Sajou, n° 149 (letter height: 25 stitches)

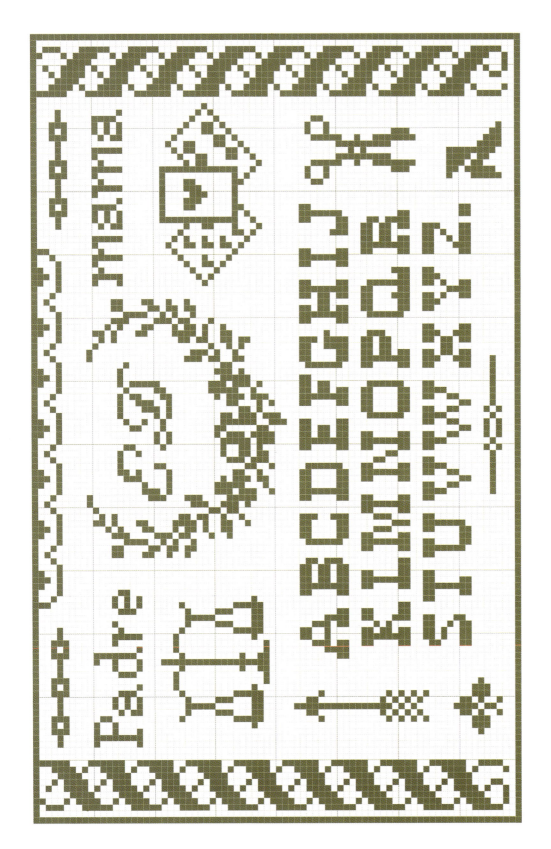

N. Alexandre, nº 98 (letter height: 9 stitches)

N. Alexandre, n° 98 (letter height: 10 stitches)

N. Alexandre, n° 144 (letter height: 27 stitches)

N. Alexandre, nº 144 (letter height: 27 stitches)

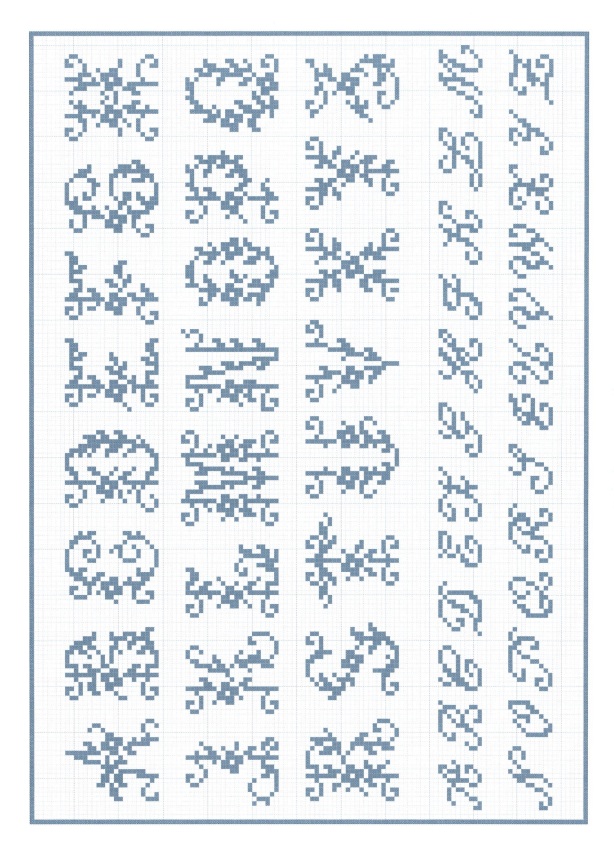

Sajou, n° 53 (letter height: first alphabet, 21 stitches; second alphabet, 10 stitches)

Sajou, n° 203 (letter height: 30 stitches)

Sajou, n° 203 (letter height: 30 stitches)

Sajou, n° 204 (letter height: 32 stitches)

Sajou, n° 204 (letter height: 45 stitches)

Sajou, n° 204 (letter height: 45 stitches)

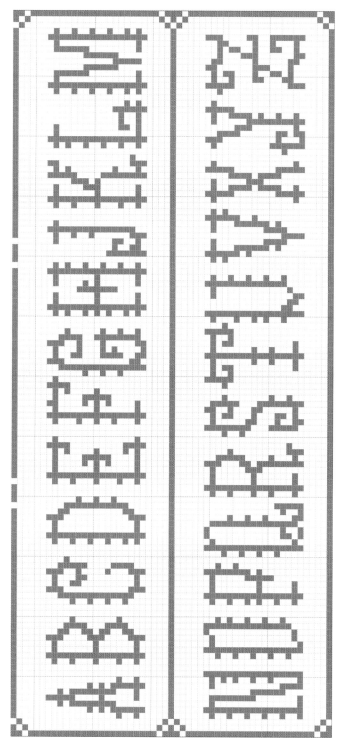

Sajou, n° 605 (letter height: large alphabet, 77 stitches; small alphabet, 21 stitches)

Sajou, n° 605 (letter height: large alphabet, 77 stitches; small alphabet, 21 stitches)

Sajou, n° 605 (letter height: large alphabet, 77 stitches; small alphabet, 21 stitches)

Sajou, n° 605 (letter height: large alphabet, 77 stitches; small alphabet, 21 stitches)

Sajou, n° 605 (letter height: large alphabet, 77 stitches; small alphabet, 23 stitches)

Sajou, n° 605 (letter height: large alphabet, 77 stitches; small alphabet, 23 stitches)

Sajou, n° 605 (letter height: large alphabet, 77 stitches; small alphabet, 23 stitches)

Sajou, n° 605 (letter height: large alphabet, 77 stitches; small alphabet, 23 stitches)

Sajou, n° 605 (letter height: large alphabet, 67 stitches; small alphabet, 33 stitches)

Sajou, n° 605 (letter height: large alphabet, 67 stitches; small alphabet, 33 stitches)

Sajou, nᵒ 605 (letter height: large alphabet, 67 stitches; small alphabet, 33 stitches)

Sajou, n° 605 (letter height: large alphabet, 67 stitches; small alphabet, 33 stitches)

Sajou, n° 605 (letter height: large alphabet, 67 stitches; small alphabet, 33 stitches)

Sajou, n° 605 (letter height: large alphabet, 67 stitches; small alphabet, 32 stitches)

Sajou, n° 605 (letter height: large alphabet, 67 stitches; small alphabet, 32 stitches)

Sajou, n° 605 (letter height: large alphabet, 67 stitches; small alphabet, 32 stitches)

Sajou, n° 654 (letter height: 41 stitches)

Sajou, n° 654 (letter height: 41 stitches)

Sajou, n° 654 (letter height: 41 stitches)

A composition inspired by various alphabets, decorating a cushion in shades of rose pink..

A lovely gift for a passionate gardener: an apron embroidered using the letter "V" from Sajou, n° 654, and Sajou, n° 3 for the other motifs.

A composition using the Sajou alphabet, n° 103.

Sajou, n° 656 (letter height: 31 stitches)

Sajou, n° 656 (letter height: 31 stitches)

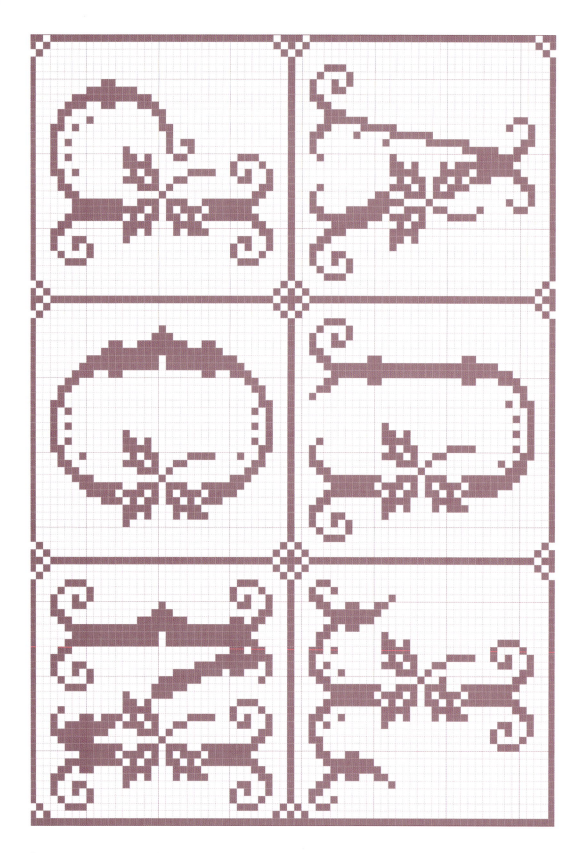

Sajou, n° 656 (letter height: 31 stitches)

Sajou, n° 656 (letter height: 40 stitches)

89   Sajou, n° 656 (letter height: 40 stitches)

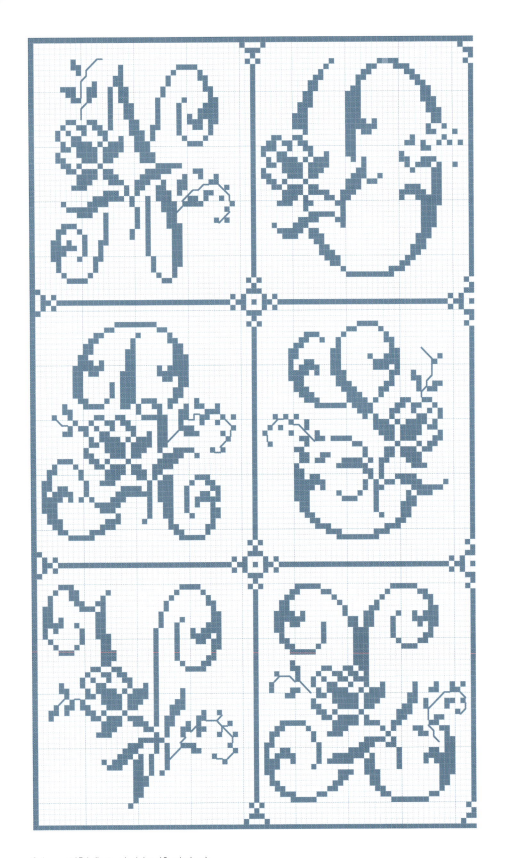

Sajou, n° 656 (letter height: 40 stitches)

Sajou, n° 656 (letter height: 40 stitches)

A. Rouyer, nº 248 (letter height: 33 stitches)

A. Rouyer, nº 248 (letter height: 33 stitches)

A. Rouyer, n° 248 (letter height: 33 stitches)

A. Rouyer, n° 248 (letter height: 33 stitches)

Sajou, n° 203 (letter height: 30 stitches)

Sajou, n° 203 (letter height: 30 stitches)

99

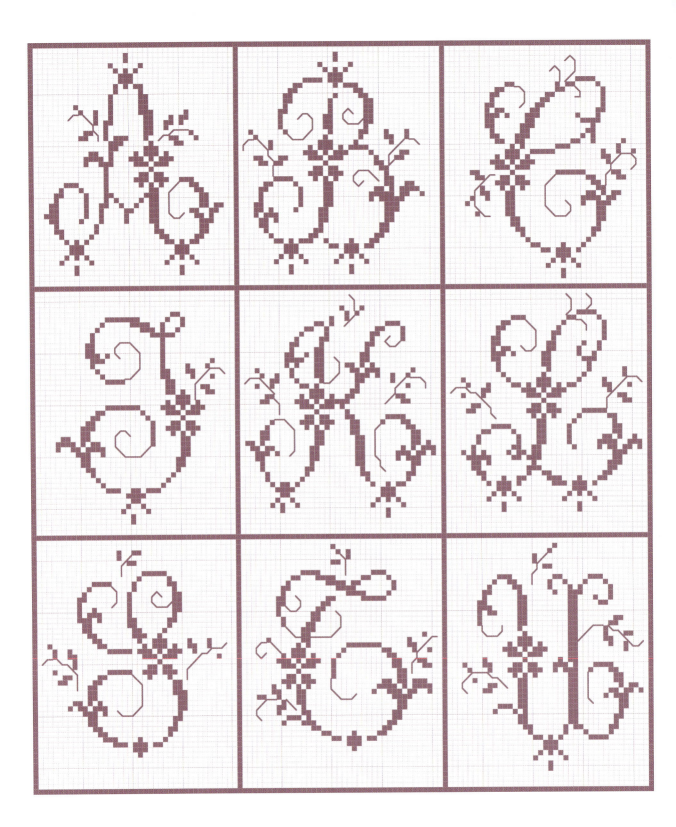

A. Rouyer, nº 152 (letter height: 43 stitches)

A. Rouyer, n° 152 (letter height: 43 stitches)

A. Rouyer, n° 152 (letter height: 43 stitches)

A series of initials taken from various alphabets, on a special fabric with squares ready for embroidering

A little bag to exude the scent of lavender in the wardrobe, this was made with aida band, sewn together on each side, embellished with a lovely piece of lace, and tied with a satin ribbon. The letter was taken from N. Alexandre, n° 229.

To create a romantic decoration, I embroidered each member of my family's initials on a heart, and arranged them in a circle (Sajou alphabet, n° 656).

N. Alexandre, n° 211 (letter height: 33 stitches; letter height with garland: 58 stitches)

N. Alexandre, n° 211 (letter height: 33 stitches; letter height with garland: 58 stitches)

N. Alexandre, n° 211 (letter height: 33 stitches; letter height with garland: 58 stitches)

Welcome message.

An original scented keyring: linen bags filled with dried lavender and embellished with a motif and a letter from the N. Alexandre alphabet, nº 211.

A. Rouyer, n° 249 (letter height: 35 stitches)

109

Ideal for serving candy or chocolates: a small tray made from red aida fabric, embroidered with green Mouliné DMC six-stranded floss, using the Sajou alphabet, n° 605.

Thanks to these personalized napkin rings, each guest will easily find their seat and can keep the embroidered gift as a memento of a festive day. I chose Sajou, n° 605, for this: I embroidered a strip of linen with a letter using one-stranded Flower Thread in white, and closed it with a small mother-of-pearl button and a button loop.

A little heart to hang at your front door to welcome guests, embroidered on an old piece of bedsheet, using three colorways of Flower Thread and A. Rouyer alphabet, n° 249.

A. Rouyer, n° 249 (letter height: 33 stitches)

A. Rouyer, n° 249 (letter height: 33 stitches)

A. Rouyer, n° 249 (letter height: 33 stitches)

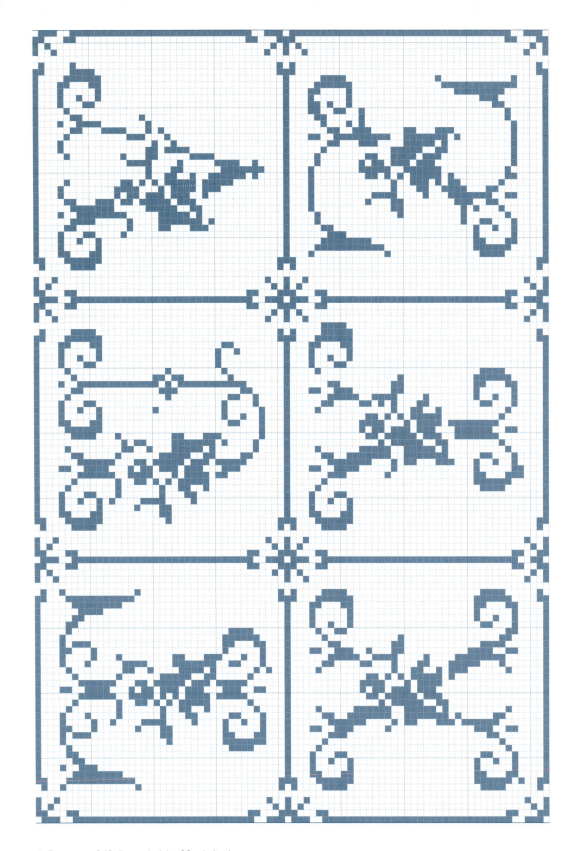

A. Rouyer, n° 249 (letter height: 33 stitches)

My daughter Émilie chose to embroider her first initial in all sorts of different styles, using A. Rouyer and N. Alexandre alphabets.

N. Alexandre, nº 211 (letter height: 48 stitches)

116

N. Alexandre, n° 211 (letter height: 48 stitches)

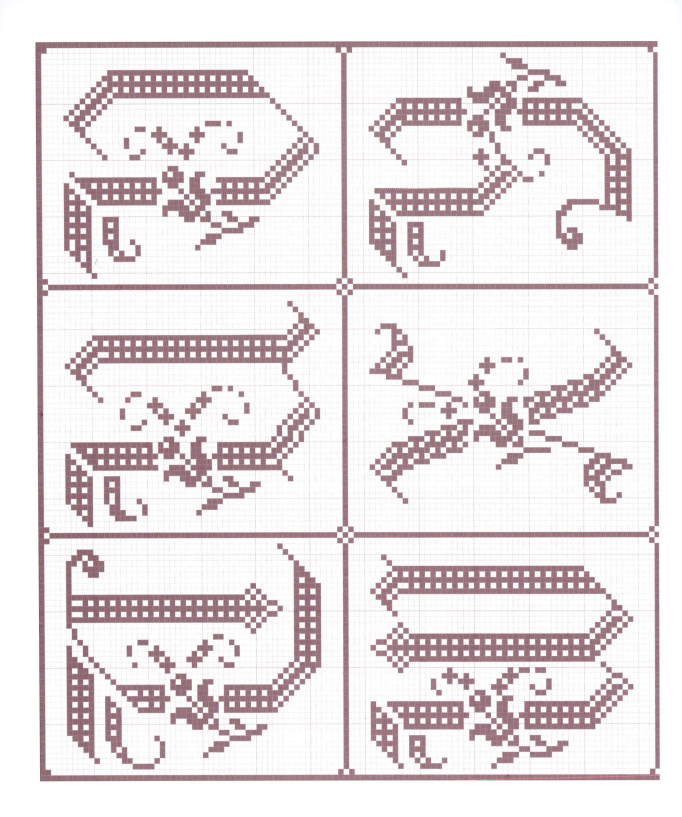

N. Alexandre, n° 211 (letter height: 48 stitches)

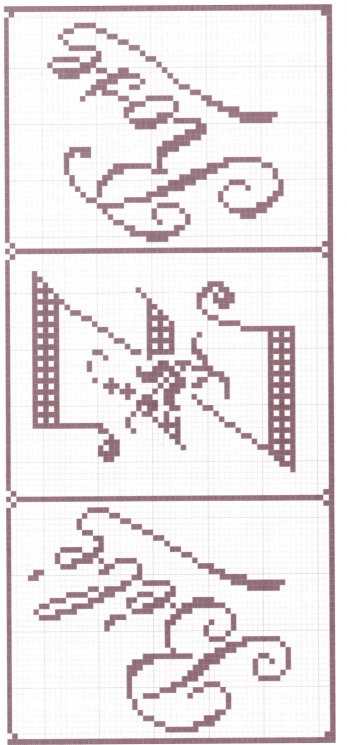

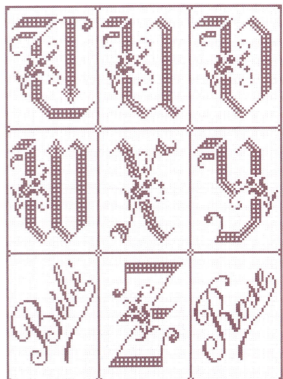

N. Alexandre, n° 211 (letter height: 48 stitches)

N. Alexandre, n° 224 (letter height: 60 stitches)

N. Alexandre, nº 224 (letter height: 60 stitches)

N. Alexandre, nº 224 (letter height: 60 stitches)

N. Alexandre, nº 224 (letter height: 60 stitches)

N. Alexandre, n° 224 (letter height: 60 stitches)

N. Alexandre, n° 224 (letter height: 60 stitches)

N. Alexandre, n° 224 (letter height: 59 stitches)

N. Alexandre, n° 224 (letter height: 59 stitches)

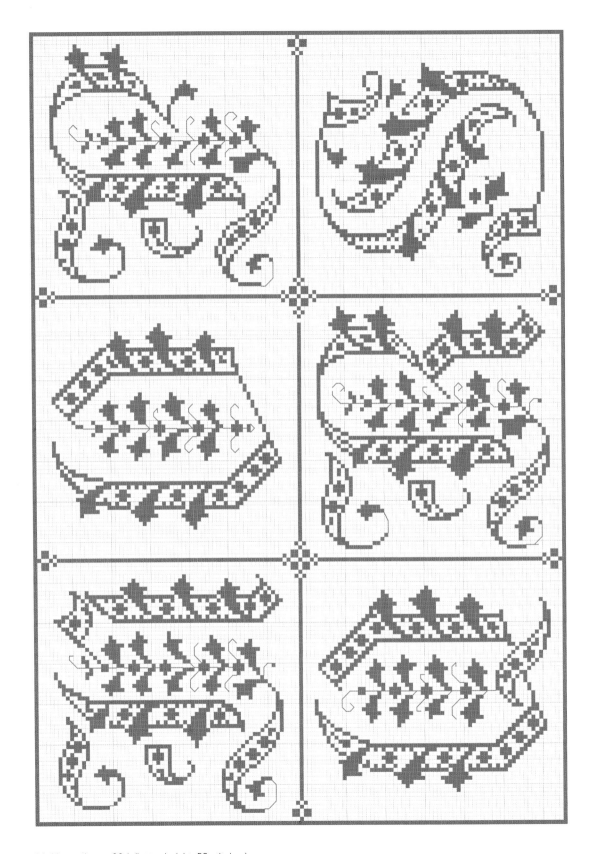

N. Alexandre, nº 224 (letter height: 59 stitches)

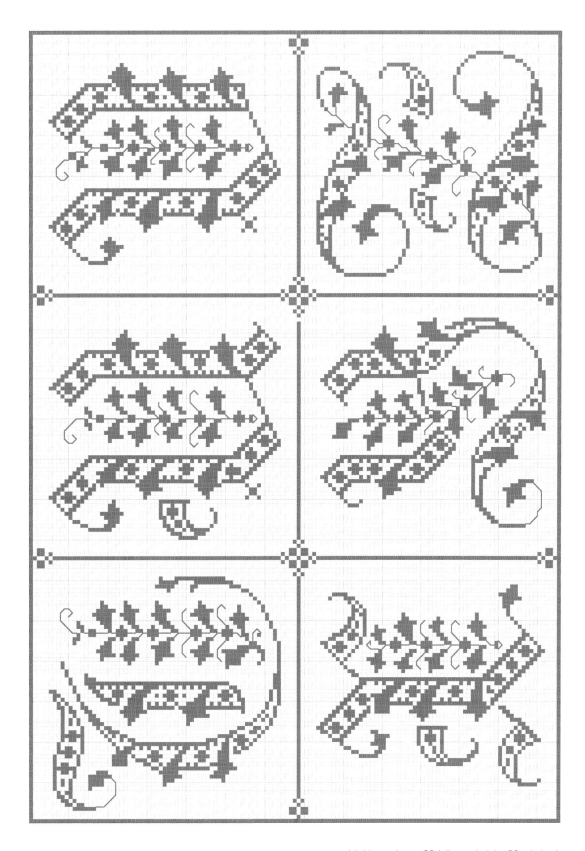

N. Alexandre, n° 224 (letter height: 59 stitches)

N. Alexandre, n° 229 (letter height: 28 stitches)

N. Alexandre, n° 229 (letter height: 28 stitches)

N. Alexandre, nº 229 (letter height: 56 stitches)

N. Alexandre, n° 229 (letter height: 56 stitches)

N. Alexandre, n° 229 (letter height: 56 stitches)

N. Alexandre, n° 229 (letter height: 56 stitches)

N. Alexandre, n° 229 (letter height: 56 stitches)

N. Alexandre, n° 229 (letter height: 56 stitches)

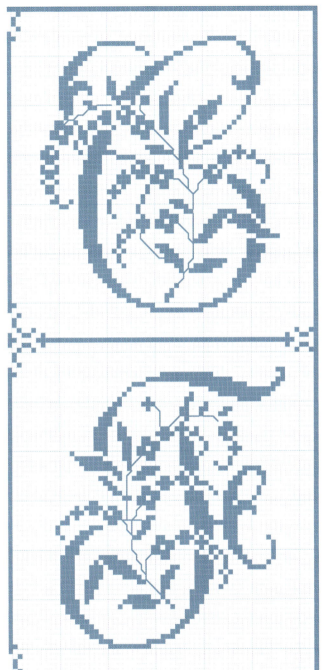

N. Alexandre, nº 229 (letter height: 56 stitches)

N. Alexandre, n° 229 (letter height: 56 stitches)

N. Alexandre, n° 229 (letter height: 56 stitches)

N. Alexandre, n° 229 (letter height: 56 stitches)

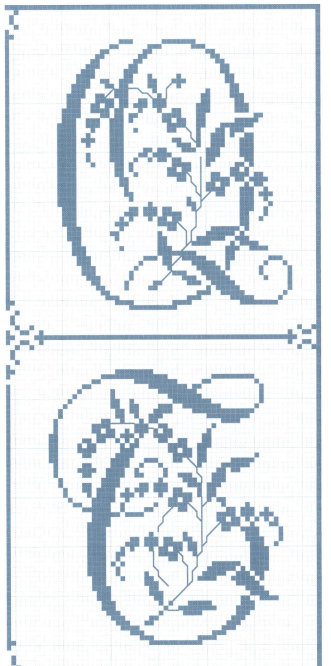

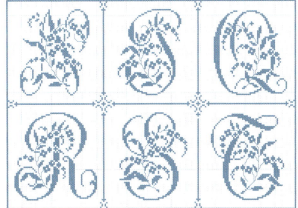

N. Alexandre, n° 229 (letter height: 56 stitches)

N. Alexandre, n° 229 (letter height: 56 stitches)

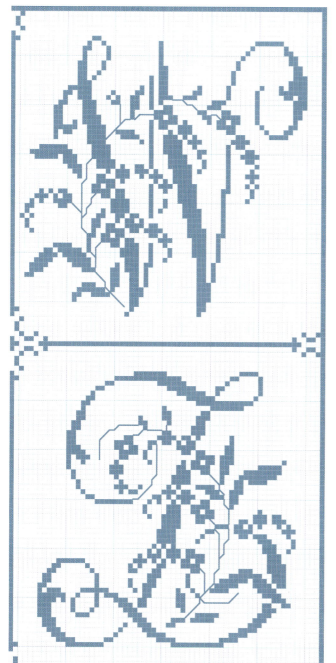

N. Alexandre, nº 229 (letter height: 56 stitches)

A. Rouyer, n° 248 (letter height: 33 stitches)

A. Rouyer, nº 248 (letter height: 33 stitches)

A. Rouyer, n° 248 (letter height: 33 stitches)

149

A. Rouyer, n° 248 (letter height: 35 stitches)

A. Rouyer, n° 248 (letter height: 35 stitches)

A. Rouyer, n° 248 (letter height: 35 stitches)

A. Rouyer, n° 248 (letter height: 35 stitches)

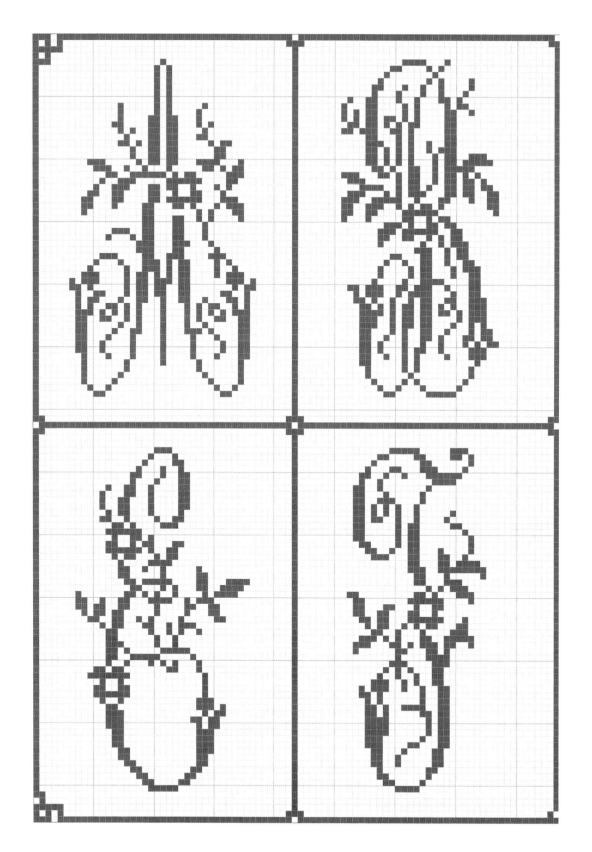

Sajou, n° 151 (letter height: 54 stitches)

Sajou, n° 151 (letter height: 54 stitches)

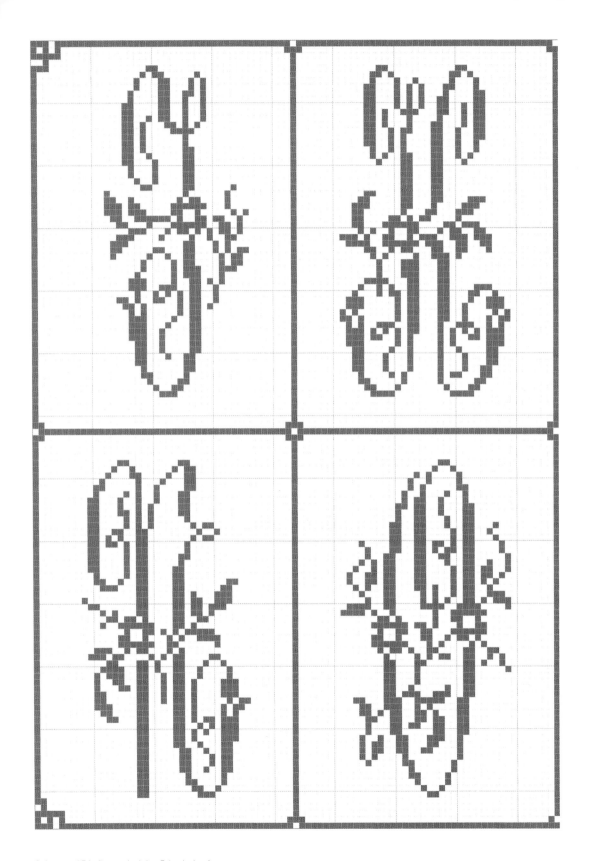

Sajou, n° 151 (letter height: 54 stitches)

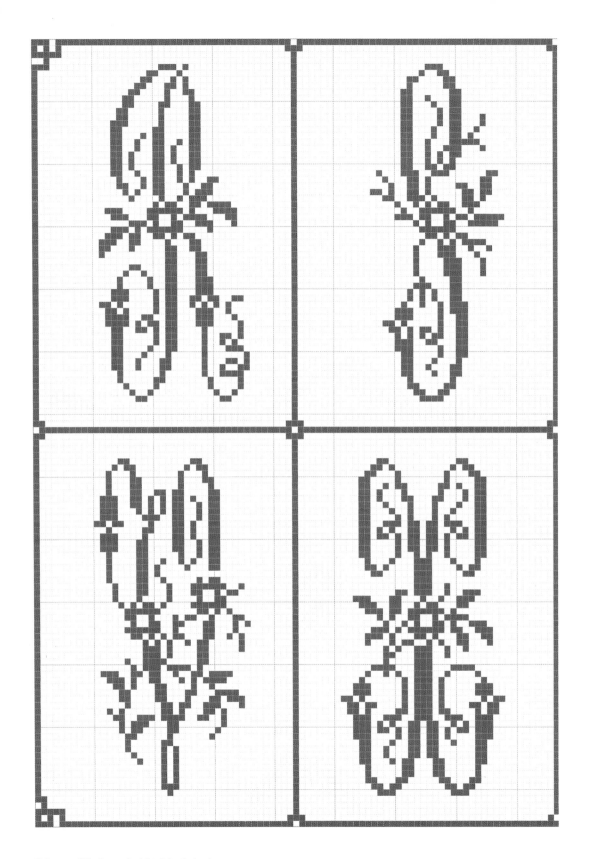

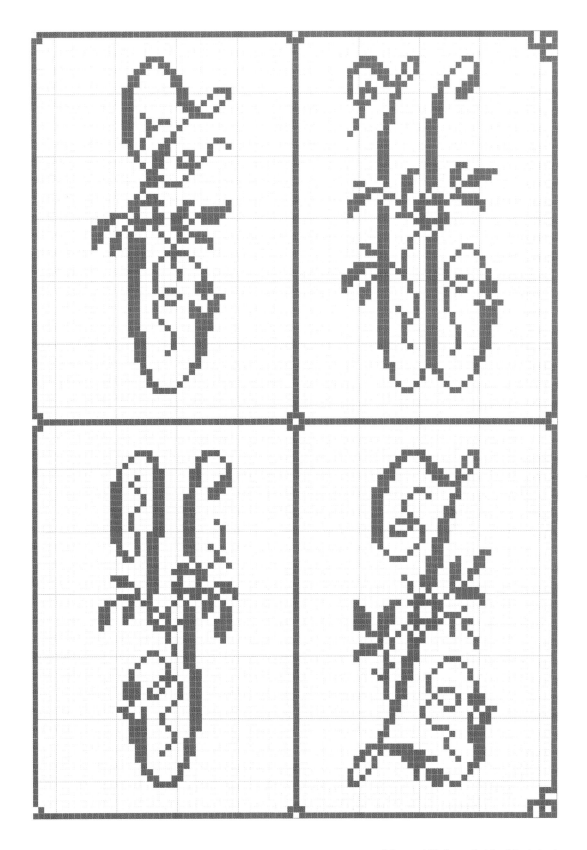

Sajou, n° 151 (letter height: 54 stitches)

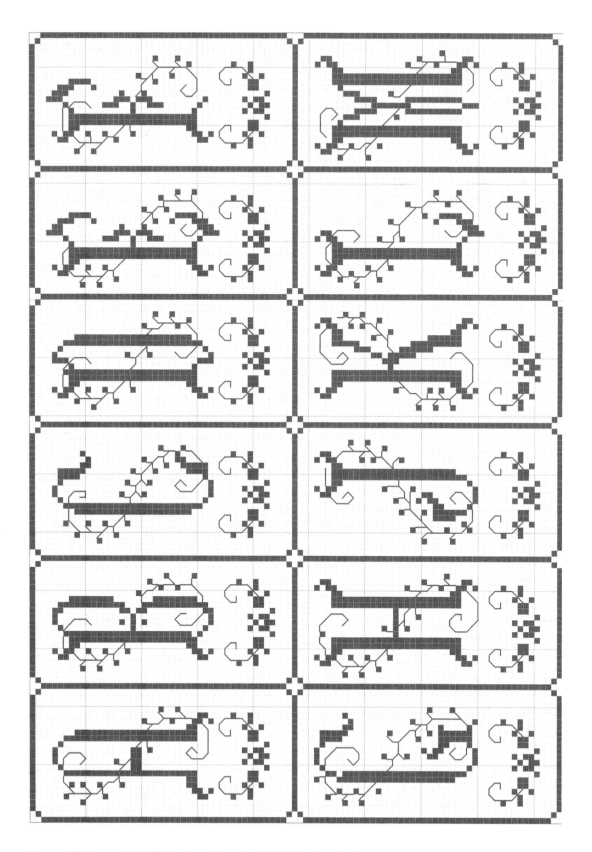

Sajou, n° 322 (letter height: 29 stitches without flourish, 40 stitches with flourish)

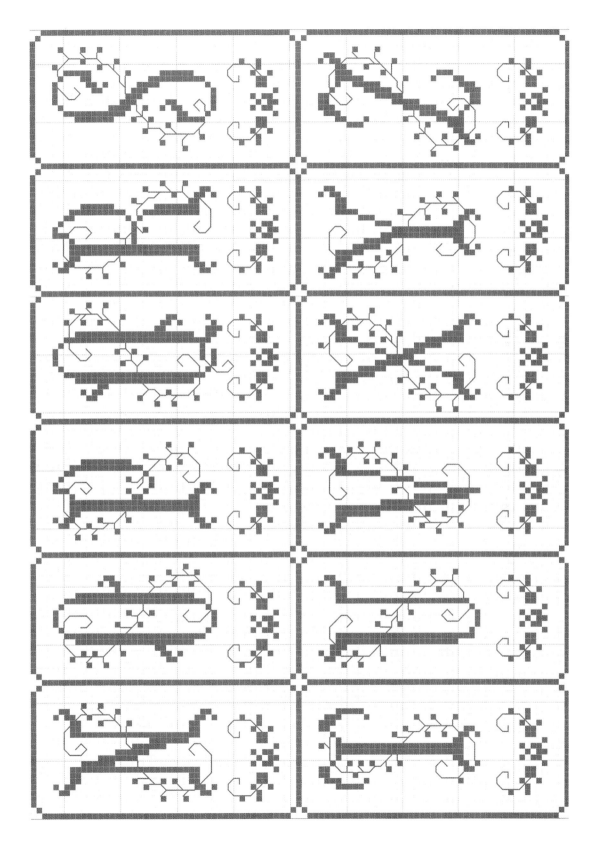

Sajou, n° 322 (letter height: 29 stitches without flourish, 40 stitches with flourish)

A. Rouyer, n° 152 (letter height: 13 stitches without flourish, 25 stitches with flourish)

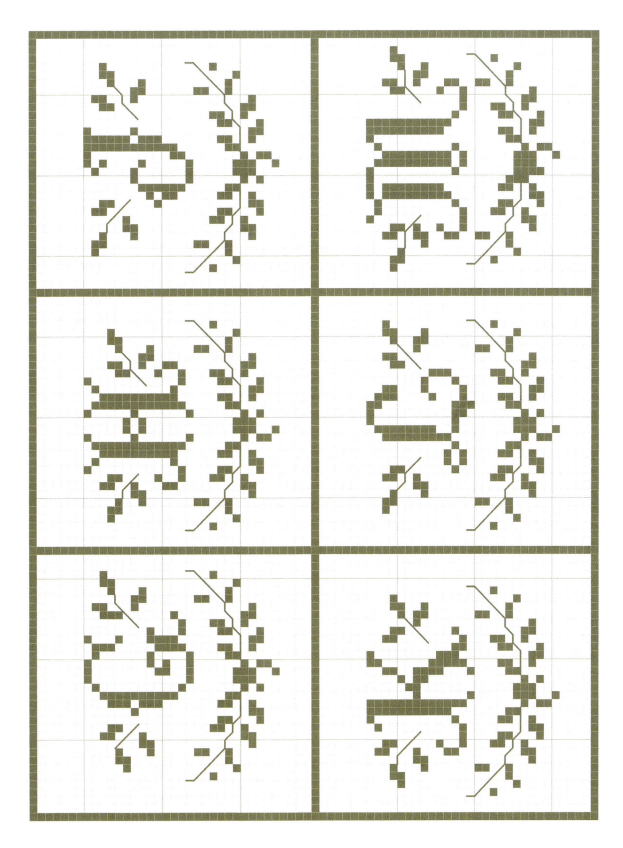

A. Rouyer, n° 152 (letter height: 13 stitches without flourish, 25 stitches with flourish)

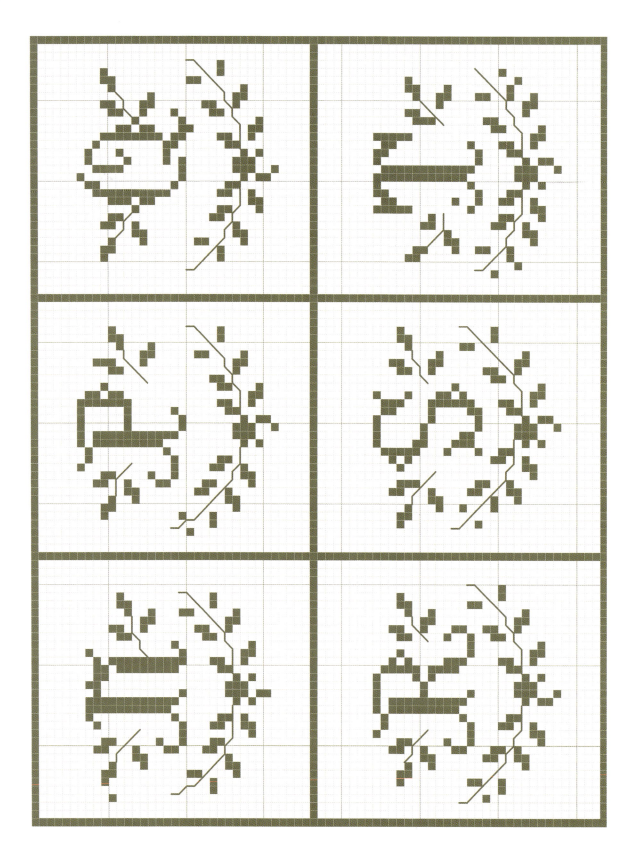

A. Rouyer, n° 152 (letter height: 13 stitches without flourish, 25 stitches with flourish)

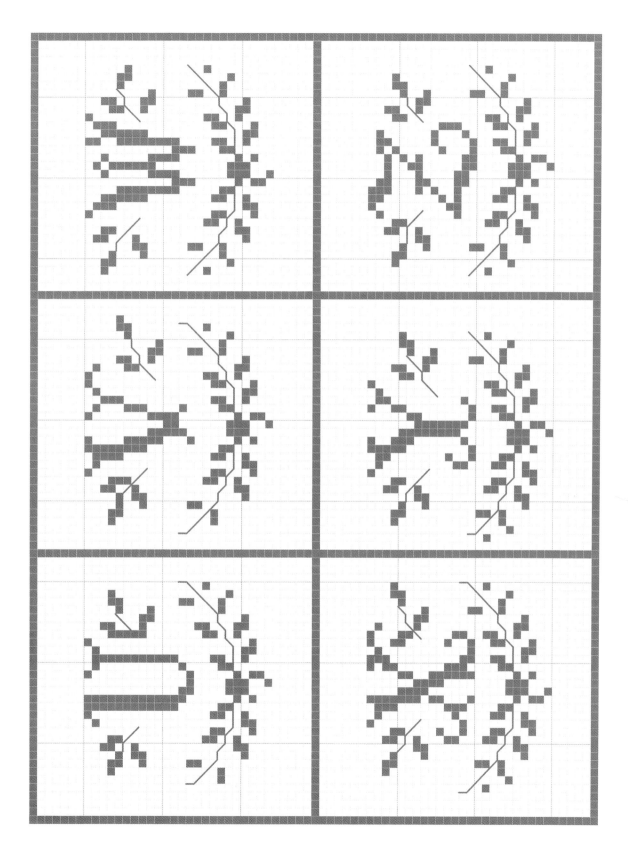

A. Rouyer, n° 152 (letter height: 13 stitches without flourish, 25 stitches with flourish)

Sajou, n° 604 (letter height: large alphabet, 67 stitches; small alphabet, 34 stitches)

Sajou, n° 604 (letter height: large alphabet, 67 stitches; small alphabet, 34 stitches)

Sajou, n° 604 (letter height: large alphabet, 67 stitches; small alphabet, 34 stitches)

Sajou, n° 604 (letter height: large alphabet, 67 stitches; small alphabet, 34 stitches)

Sajou, n° 604 (letter height: large alphabet, 67 stitches; small alphabet, 34 stitches)

Sajou, n° 604 (letter height: large alphabet, 67 stitches; small alphabet, 34 stitches)

Sajou, n° 604 (letter height: large alphabet, 67 stitches; small alphabet, 34 stitches)

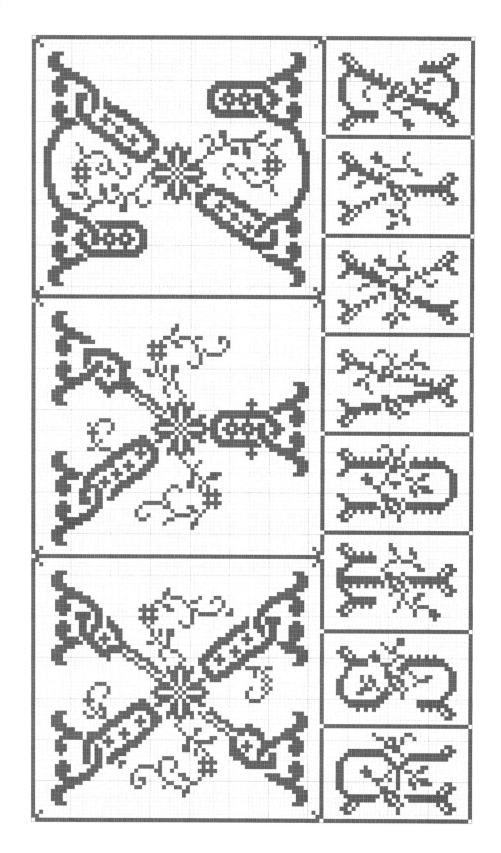

Sajou, n° 604 (letter height: large alphabet, 67 stitches; small alphabet, 34 stitches)

Sajou, n° 653 (letter height: 31 stitches)

Sajou, n° 653 (letter height: 29 stitches)

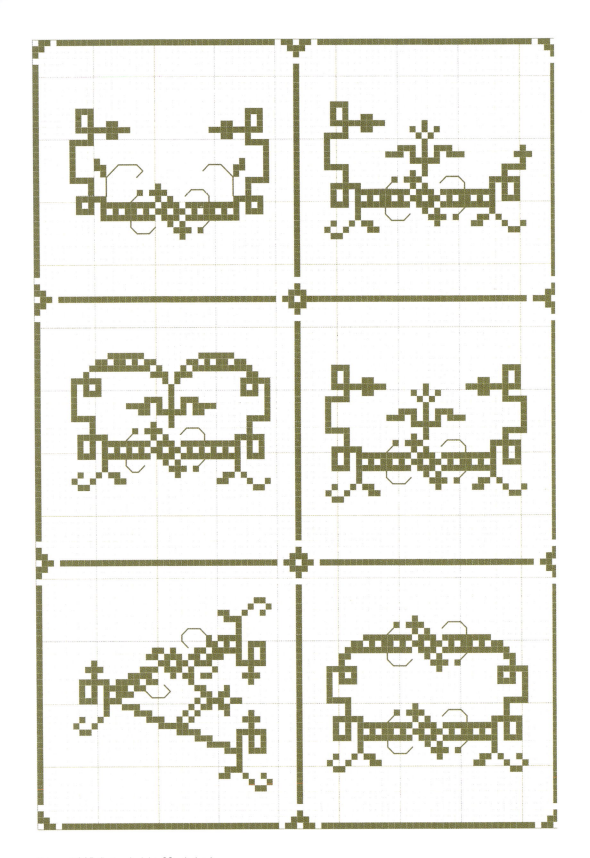

Sajou, n° 205 (letter height: 33 stitches)

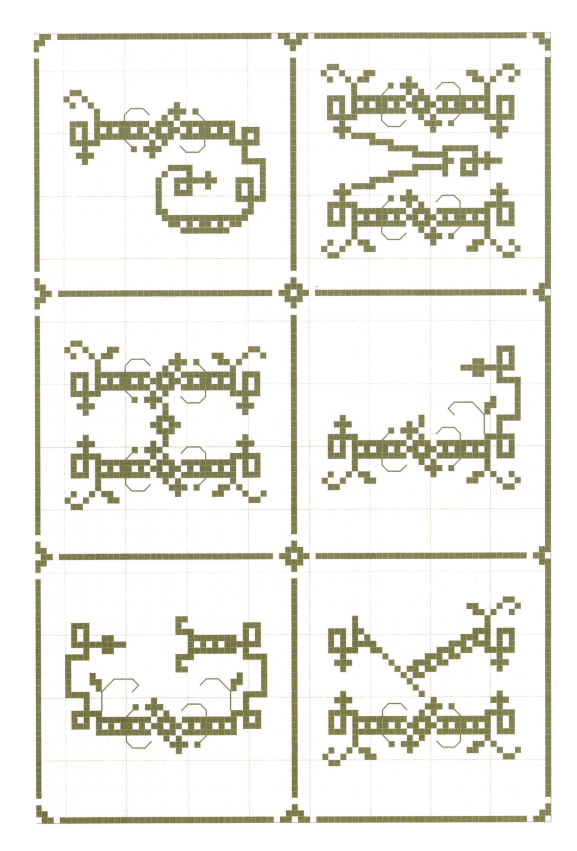

Sajou, n° 205 (letter height: 33 stitches)

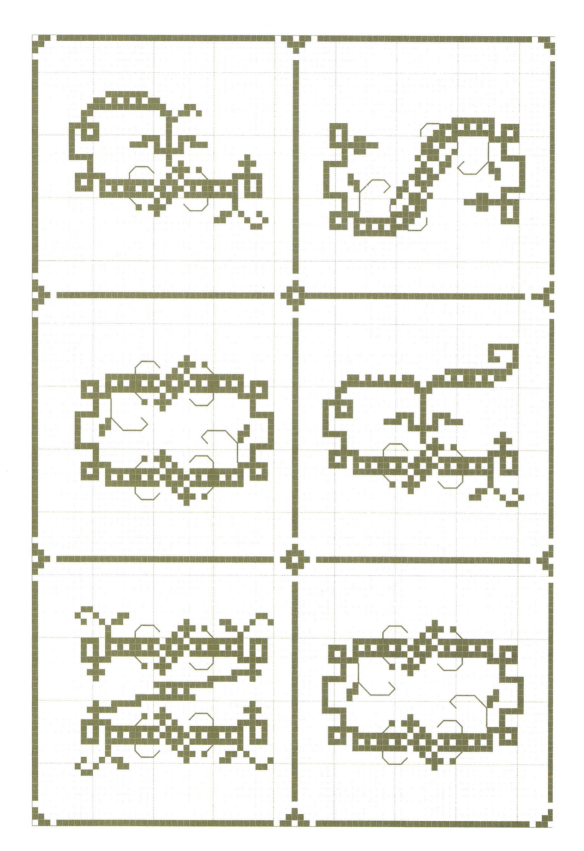

Sajou, n° 205 (letter height: 33 stitches)

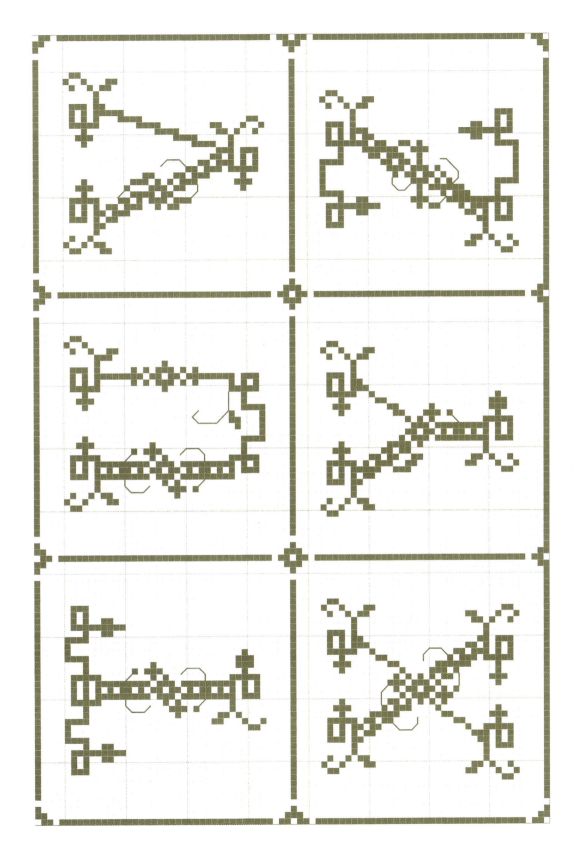

Sajou, n° 205 (letter height: 33 stitches)

Sajou, n° 205 (letter height: 33 stitches)

185

Sajou, n° 205 (letter height: 33 stitches)

Sajou, n° 606 (letter height: large alphabet, 66 stitches; small alphabet, 33 stitches)

Sajou, n° 606 (letter height: large alphabet, 66 stitches; small alphabet, 33 stitches)

Sajou, n° 606 (letter height: large alphabet, 66 stitches; small alphabet, 33 stitches)

Sajou, n° 606 (letter height: large alphabet, 66 stitches; small alphabet, 33 stitches)

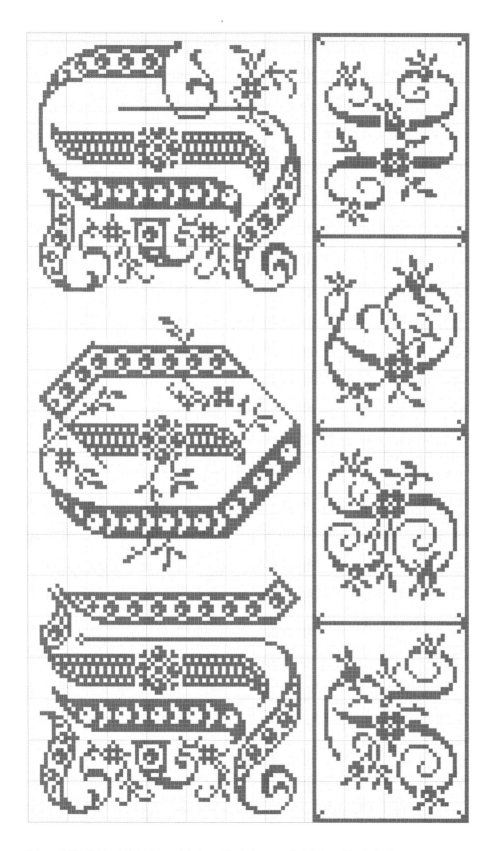

Sajou, n° 606 (letter height: large alphabet, 66 stitches; small alphabet, 33 stitches)

Sajou, n° 606 (letter height: large alphabet, 66 stitches; small alphabet, 33 stitches)

Sajou, n° 606 (letter height: large alphabet, 66 stitches; small alphabet, 33 stitches)

Sajou, n° 606 (letter height: large alphabet, 66 stitches; small alphabet, 33 stitches)

Sajou, n° 323 (letter height: 28 stitches)

Sajou, n° 323 (letter height: 28 stitches)

197

Sajou, n° 325 (letter height: 57 stitches)

Sajou, n° 325 (letter height: 57 stitches)

Sajou, n° 325 (letter height: 57 stitches)

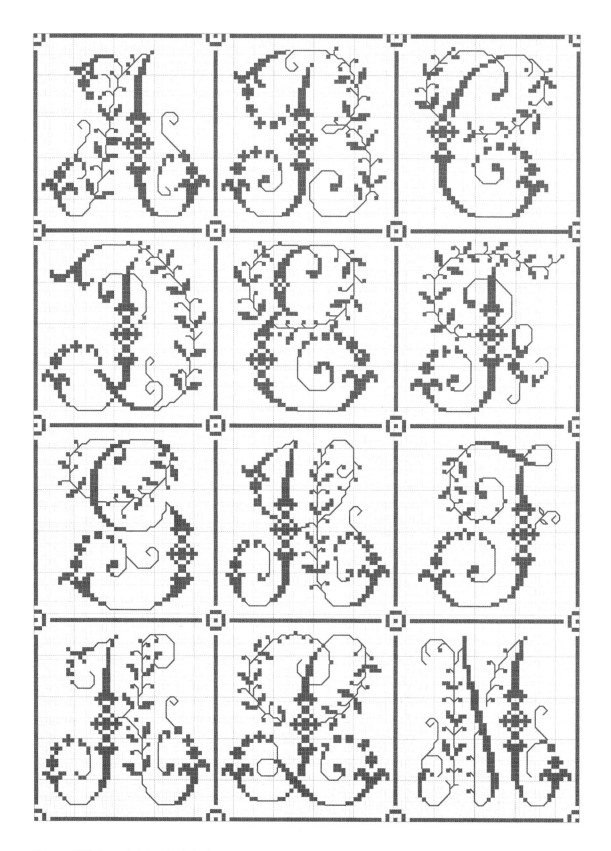

Sajou, n° 323 (letter height: 41 stitches)

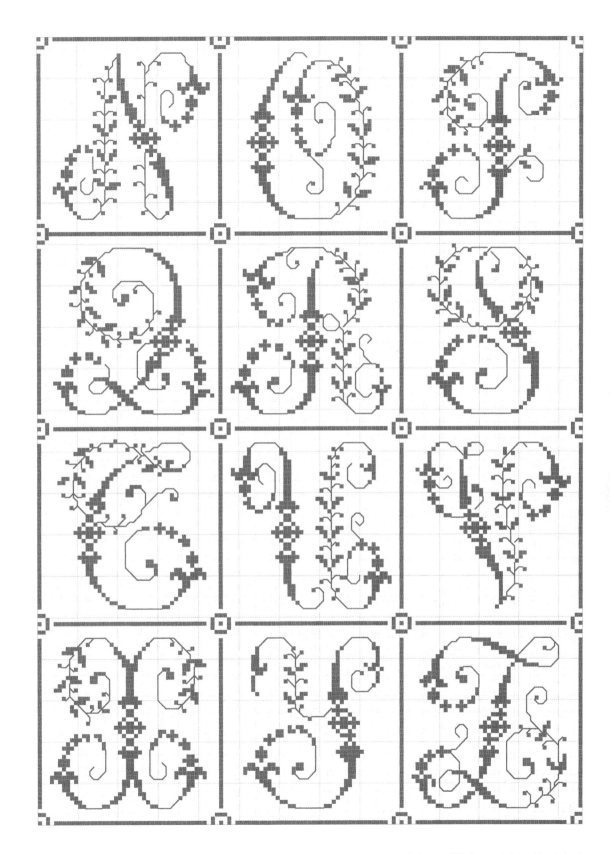

Sajou, n° 323 (letter height: 41 stitches)

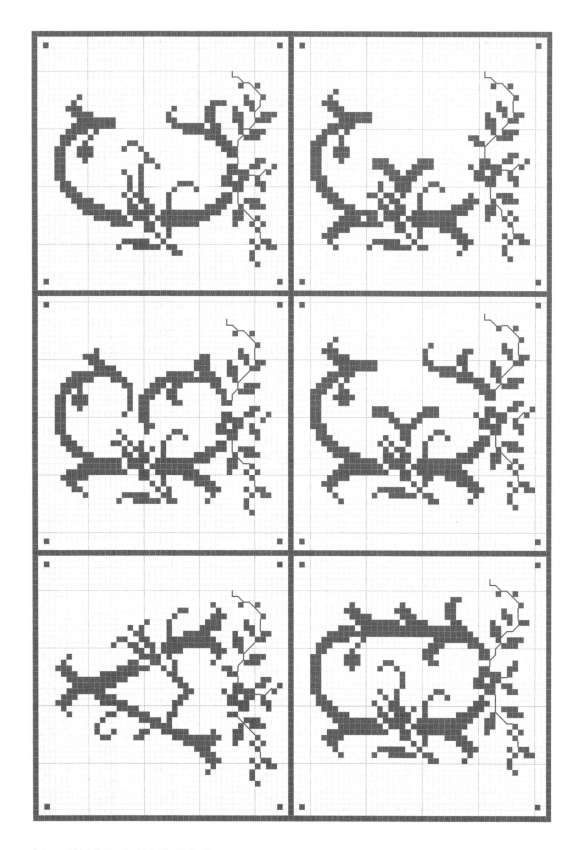

Sajou, n° 322 (letter height: 40 stitches)

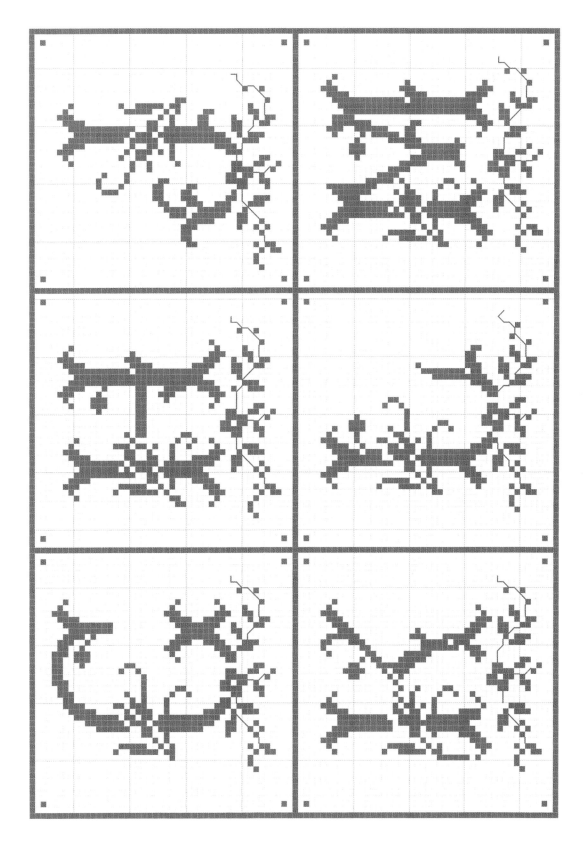

Sajou, n° 322 (letter height: 40 stitches)

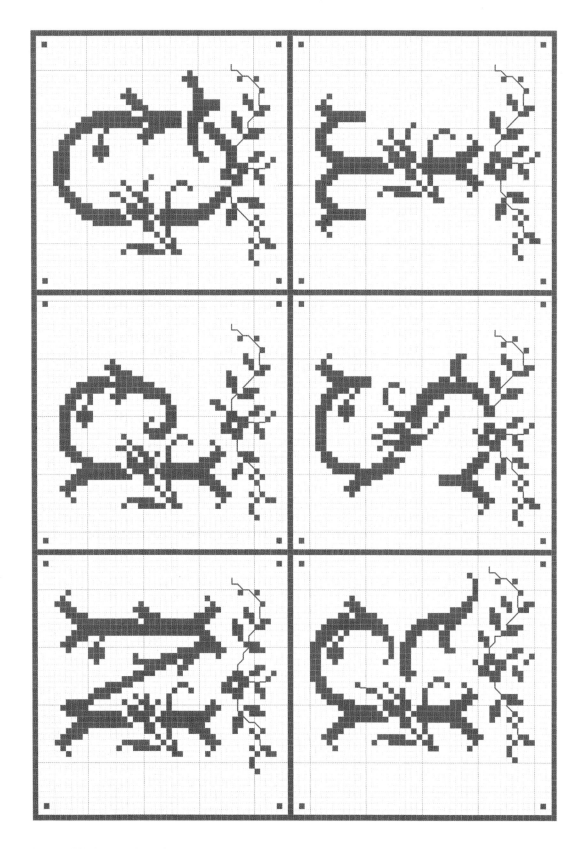

Sajou, n° 322 (letter height: 40 stitches)

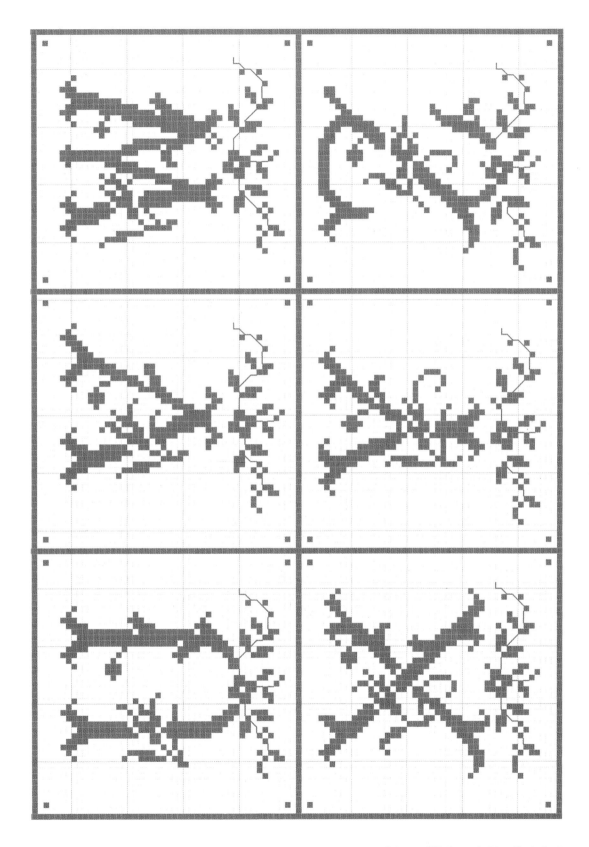

209

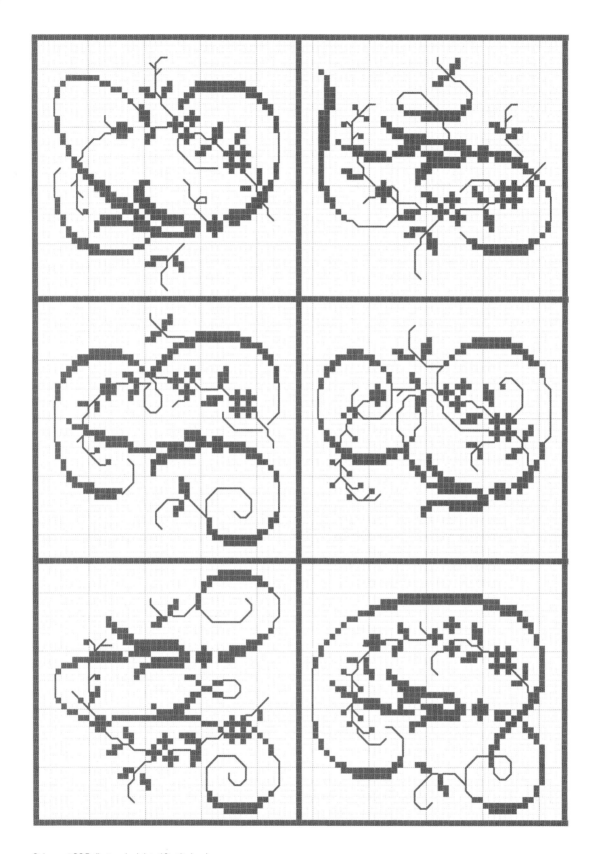

Sajou, n° 325 (letter height: 40 stitches)

Sajou, n° 325 (letter height: 40 stitches)

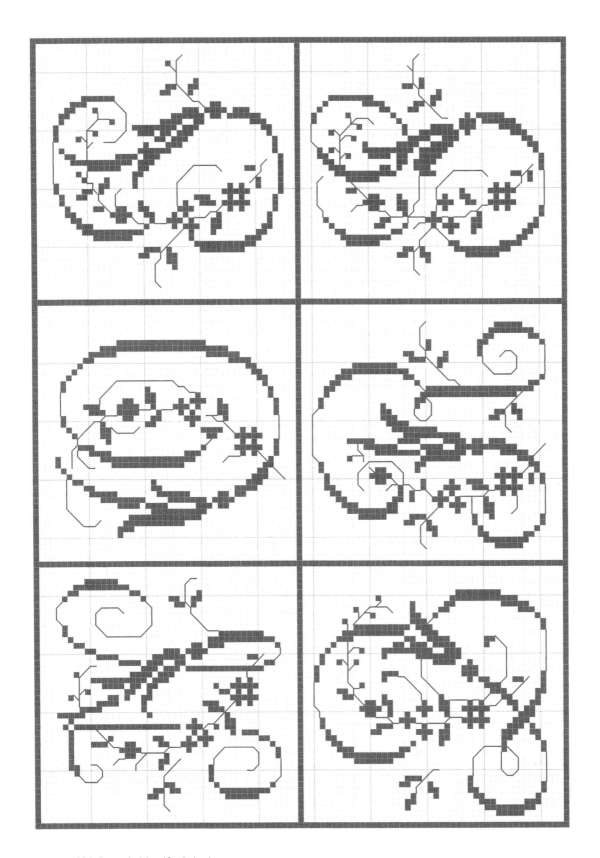

Sajou, n° 325 (letter height: 40 stitches)

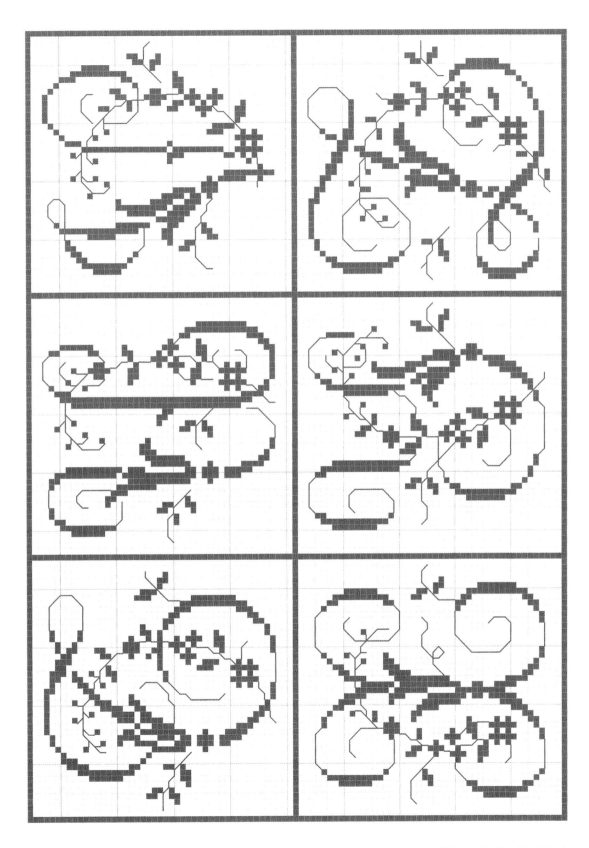

Sajou, n° 325 (letter height: 40 stitches)

Sajou, n° 322 (letter height: 40 stitches)

Sajou, n° 322 (letter height: 40 stitches)

Sajou, n° 322 (letter height: 40 stitches)

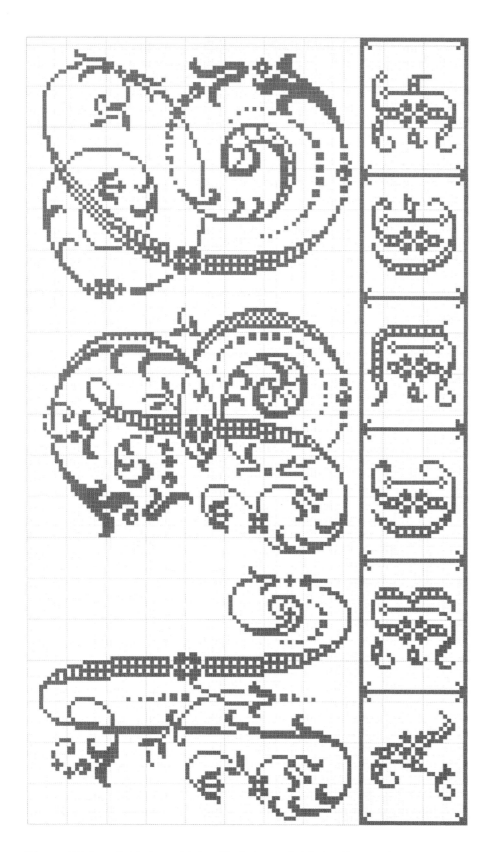

Sajou, n° 606 (letter height: large alphabet, 80 stitches; small alphabet, 20 stitches)

Sajou, n° 606 (letter height: large alphabet, 80 stitches; small alphabet, 20 stitches)

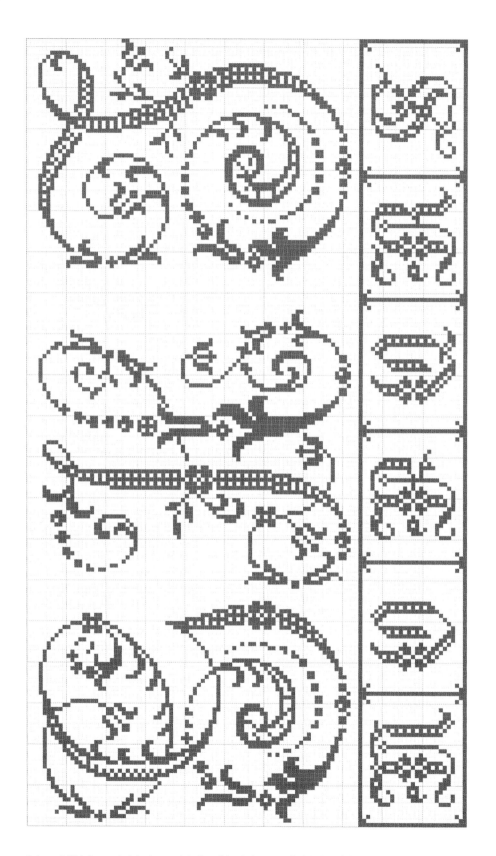

Sajou, n° 606 (letter height: large alphabet, 80 stitches; small alphabet, 20 stitches)

Sajou, n° 606 (letter height: large alphabet, 80 stitches; small alphabet, 20 stitches)

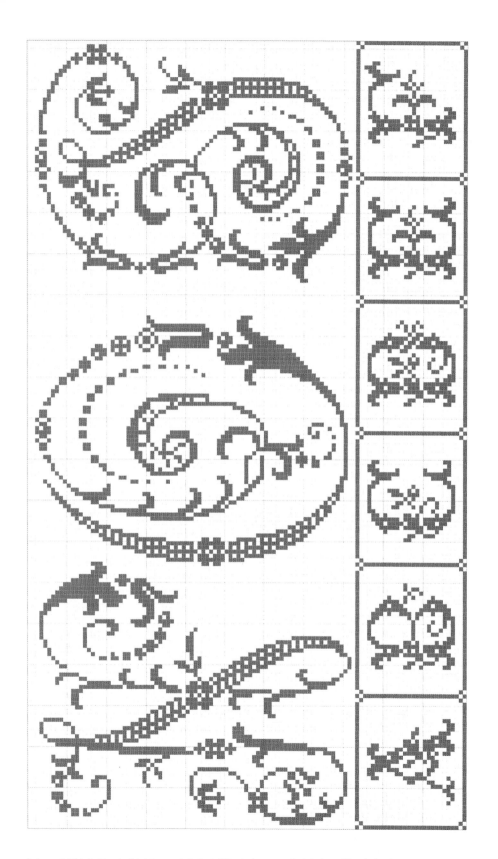

Sajou, n° 606 (letter height: large alphabet, 80 stitches; small alphabet, 20 stitches)

Sajou, n° 606 (letter height: large alphabet, 80 stitches; small alphabet, 20 stitches)

Sajou, n° 606 (letter height: large alphabet, 80 stitches; small alphabet, 20 stitches)

Sajou, n° 606 (letter height: large alphabet, 80 stitches; small alphabet, 20 stitches)

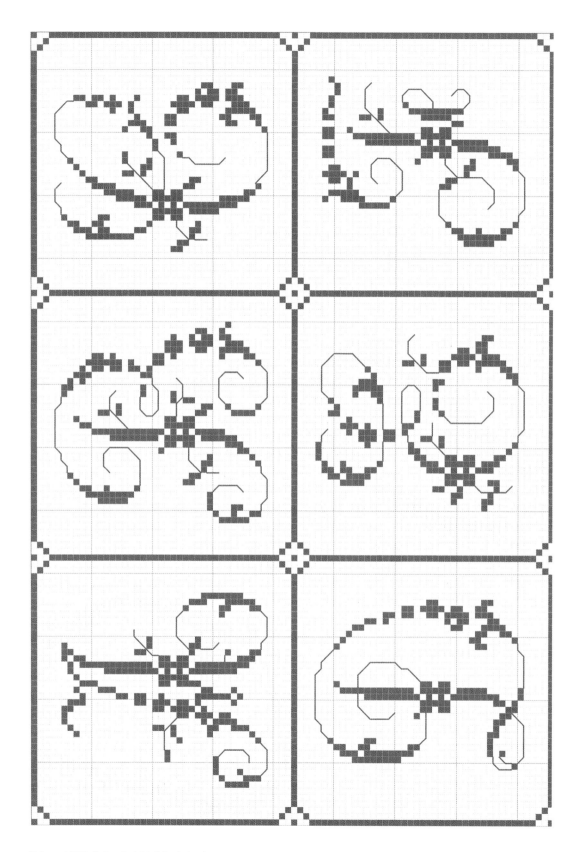

Sajou, n° 205 (letter height: 34 stitches)

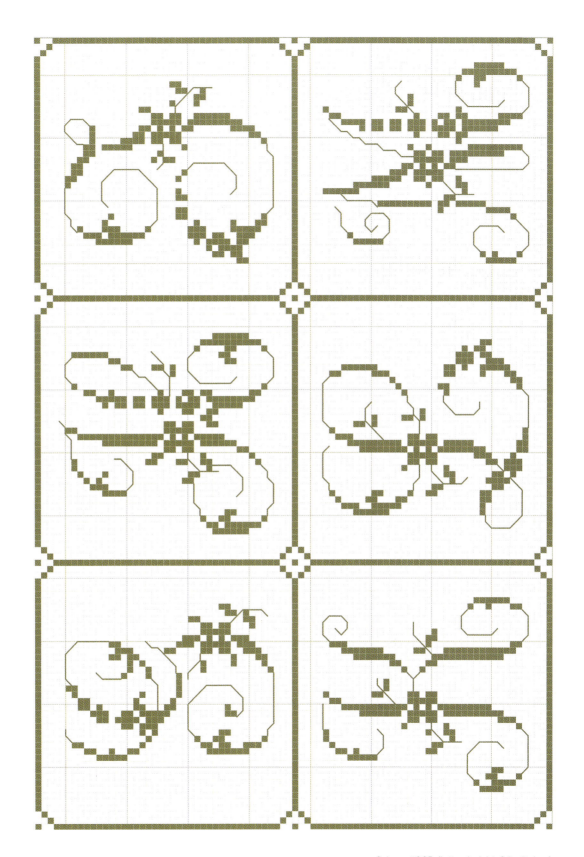

Sajou, n° 205 (letter height: 34 stitches)

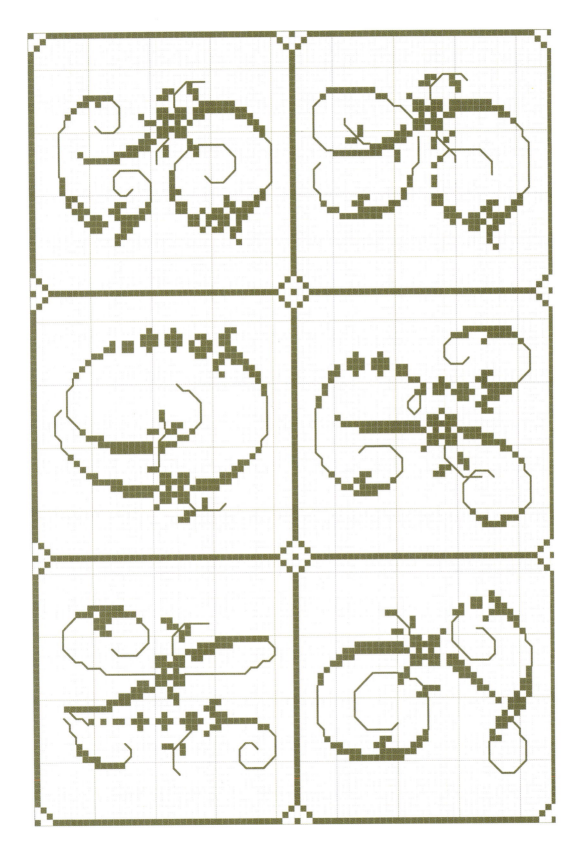

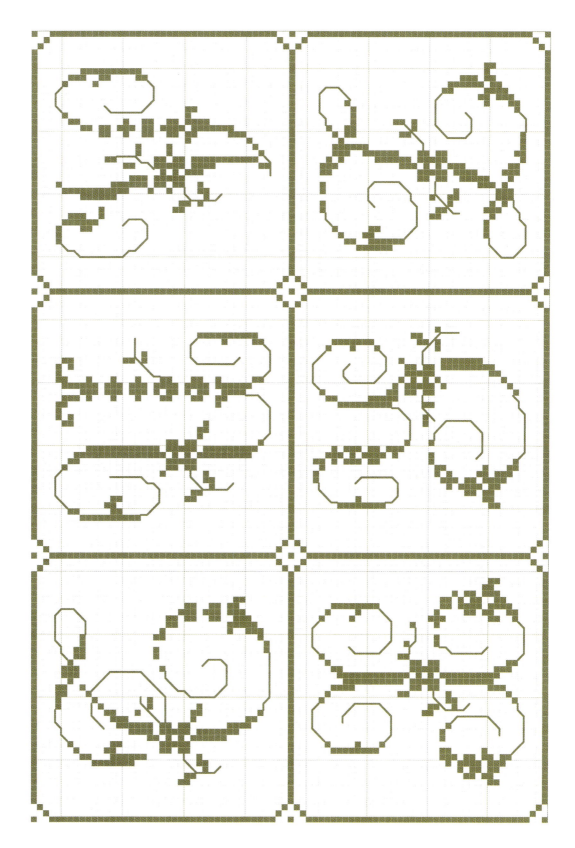

Sajou, n° 205 (letter height: 34 stitches)

Sajou, n° 362 (letter height: 35 stitches)

Sajou, n° 362 (letter height: 35 stitches)

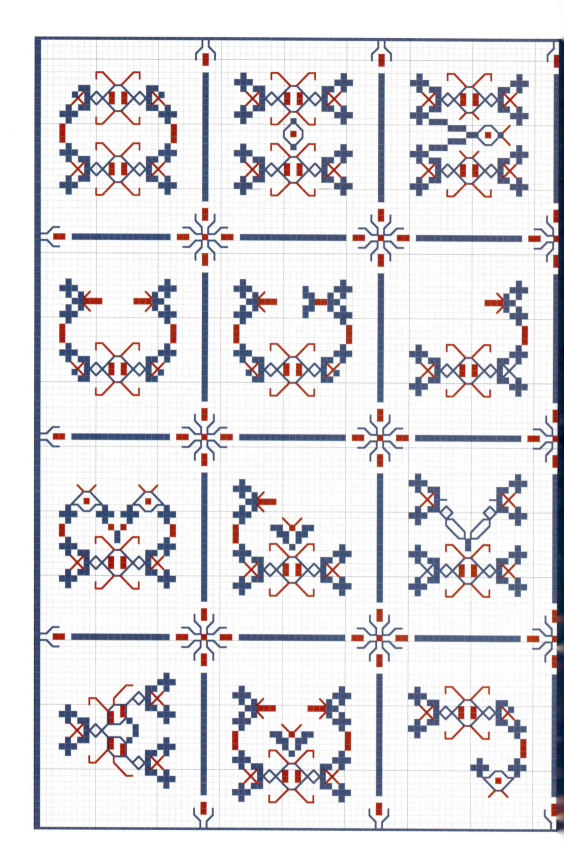

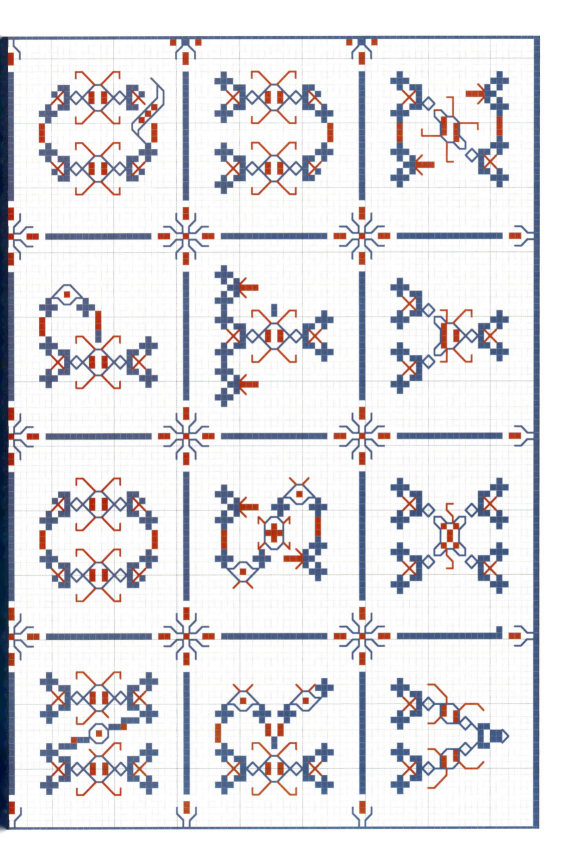

233

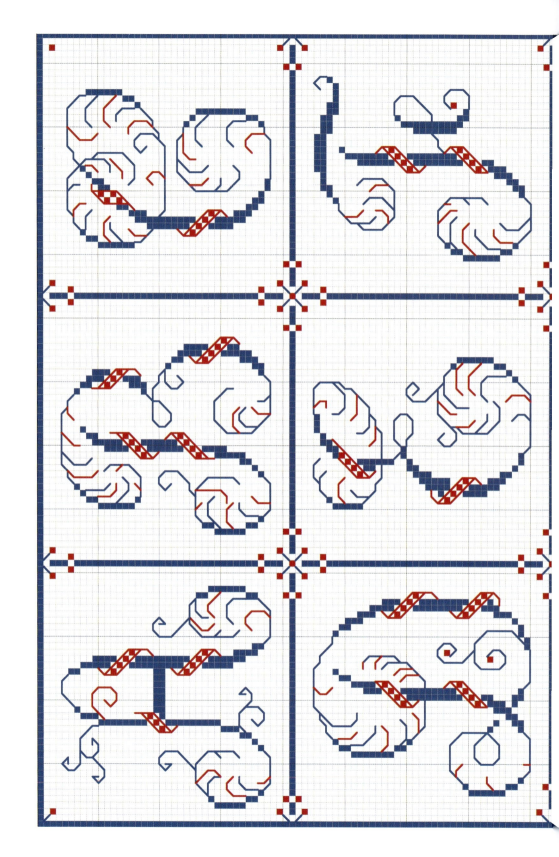

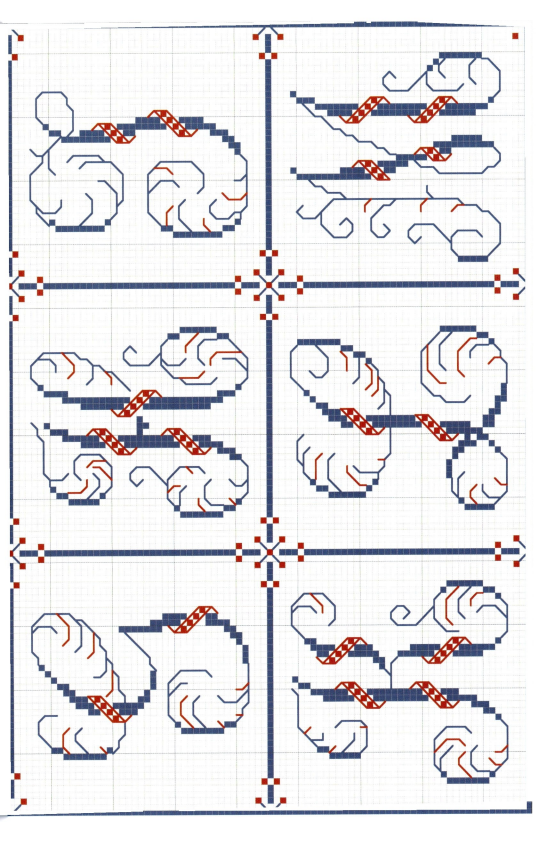

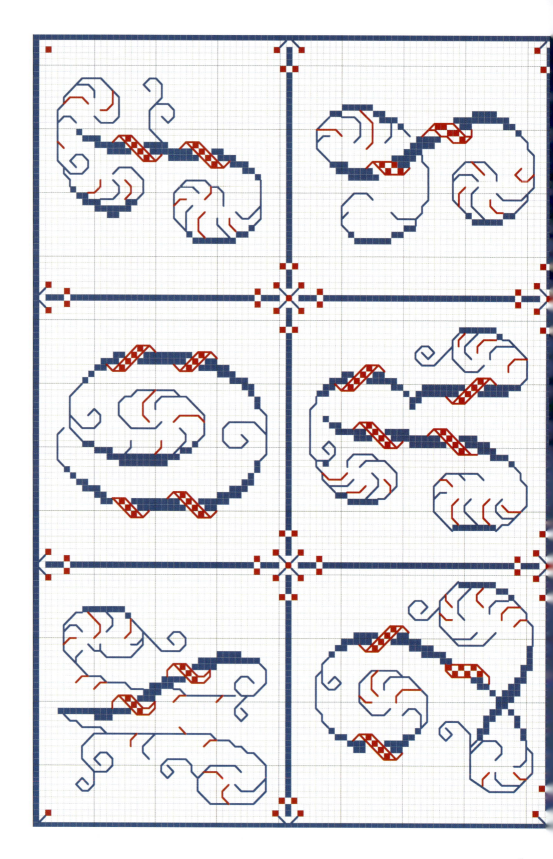

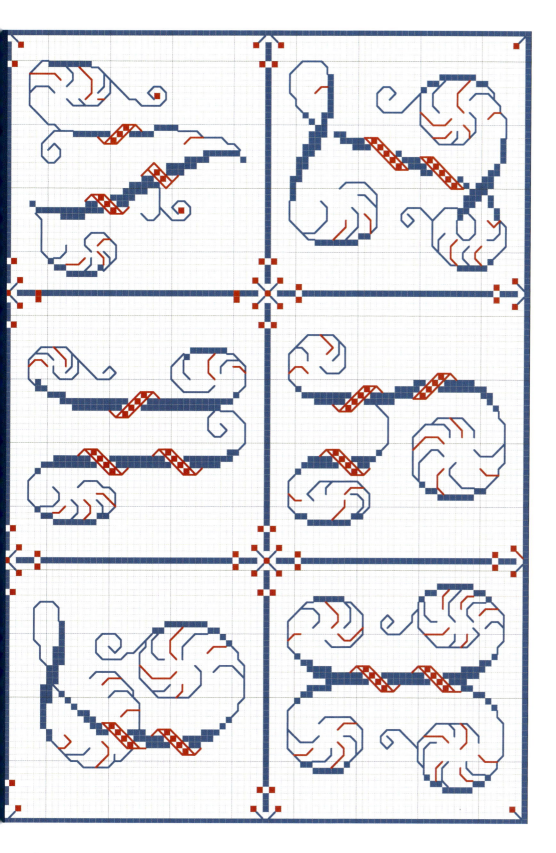

239

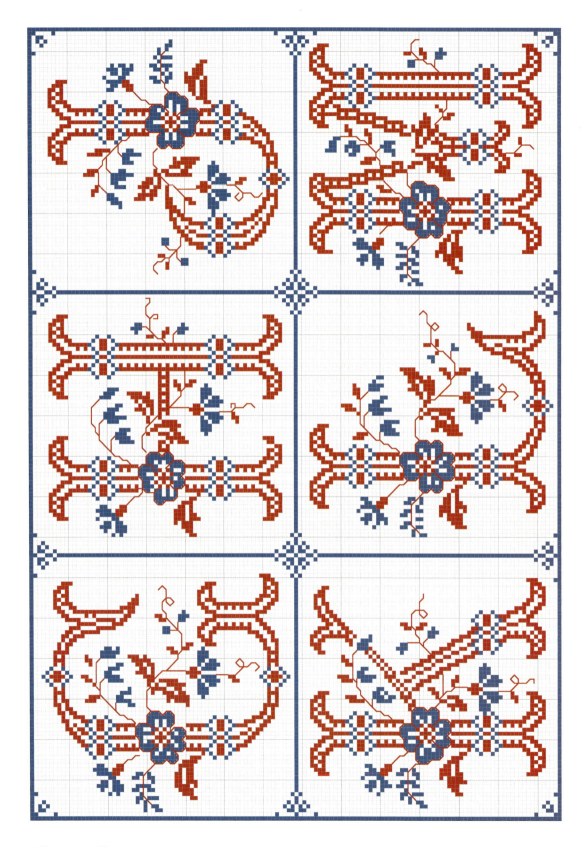

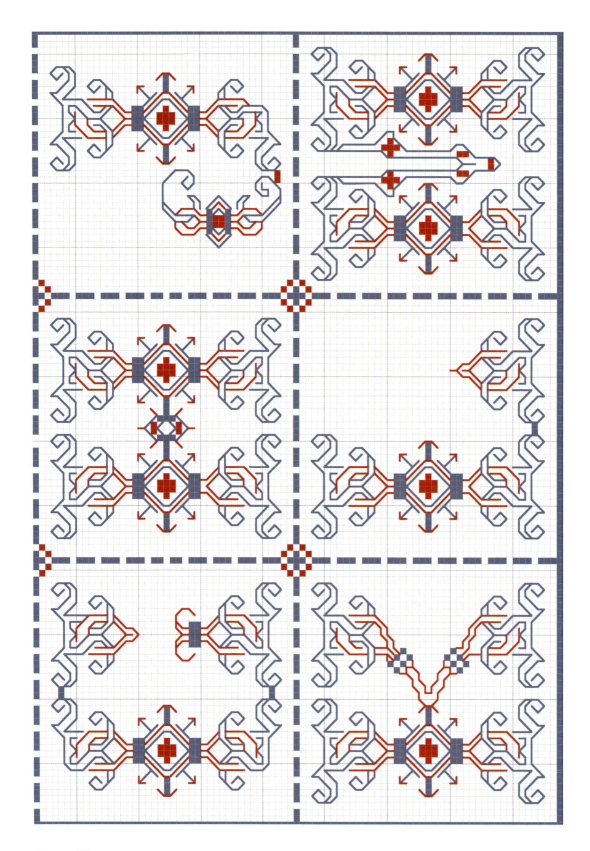

245

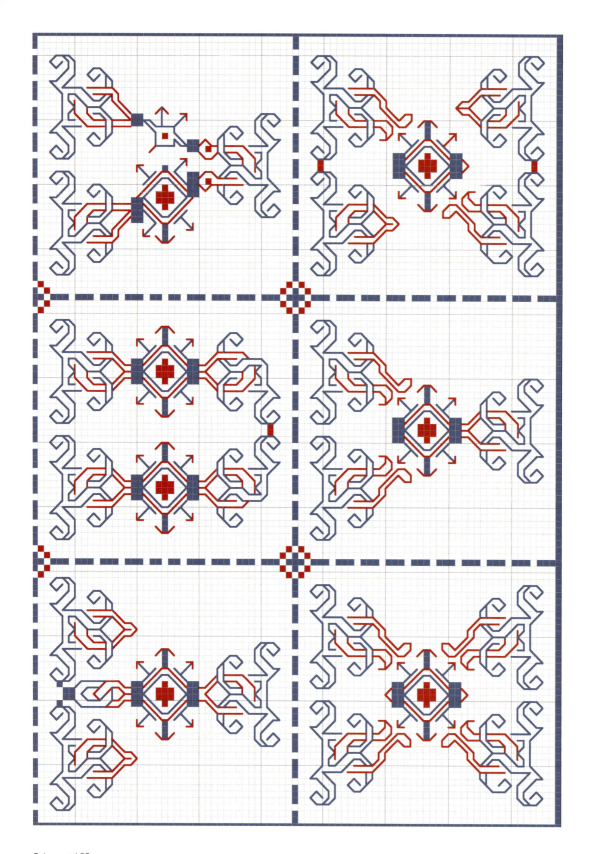

Sajou, n° 182

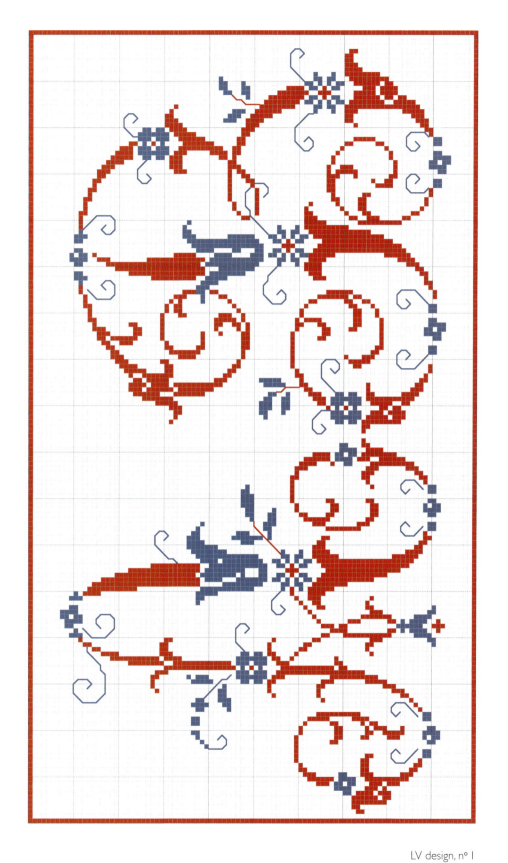

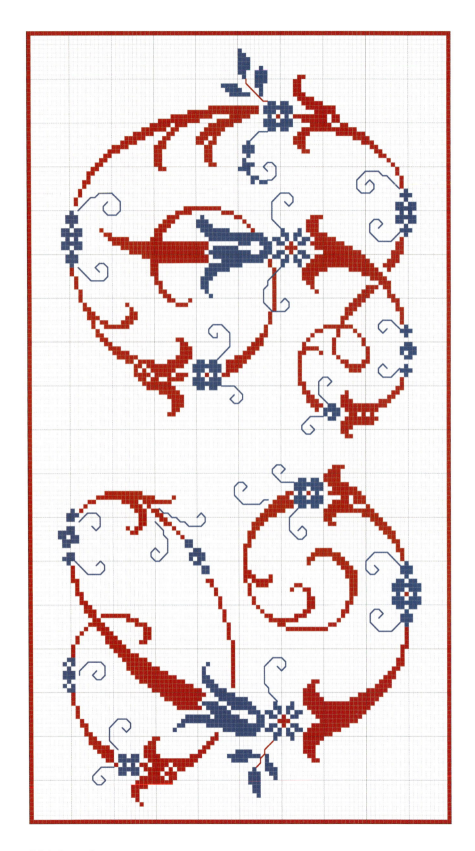

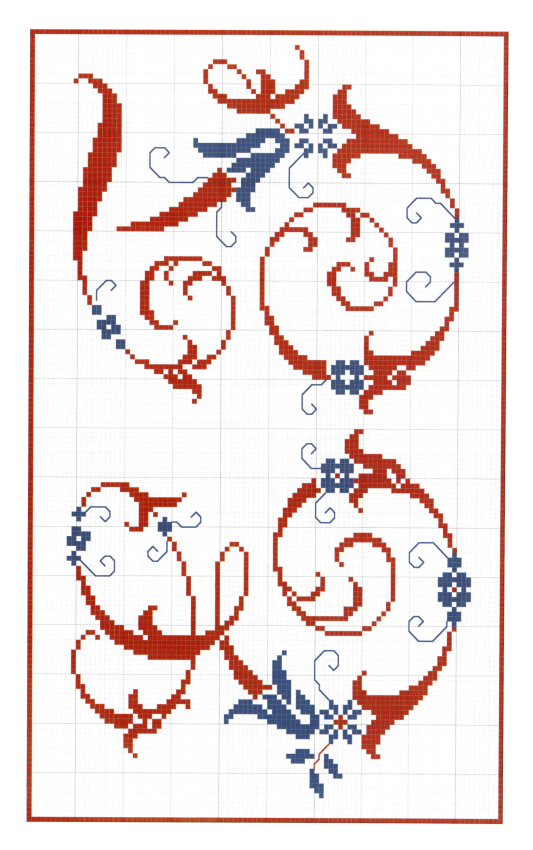

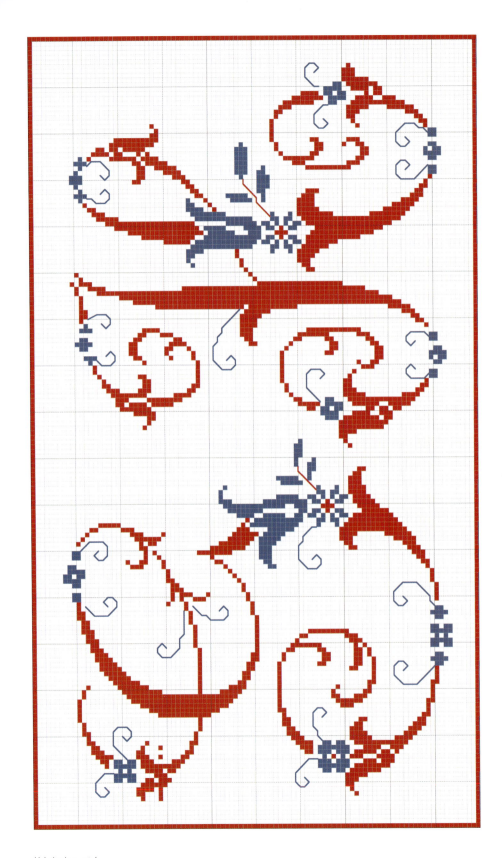

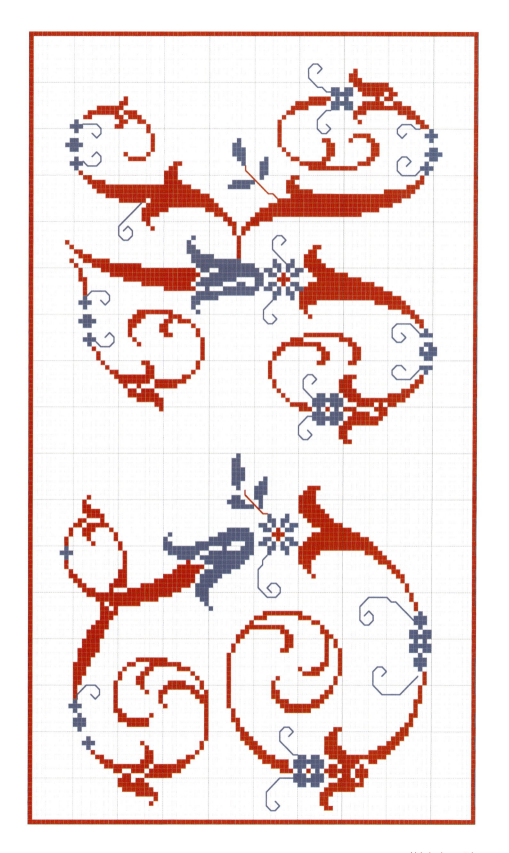

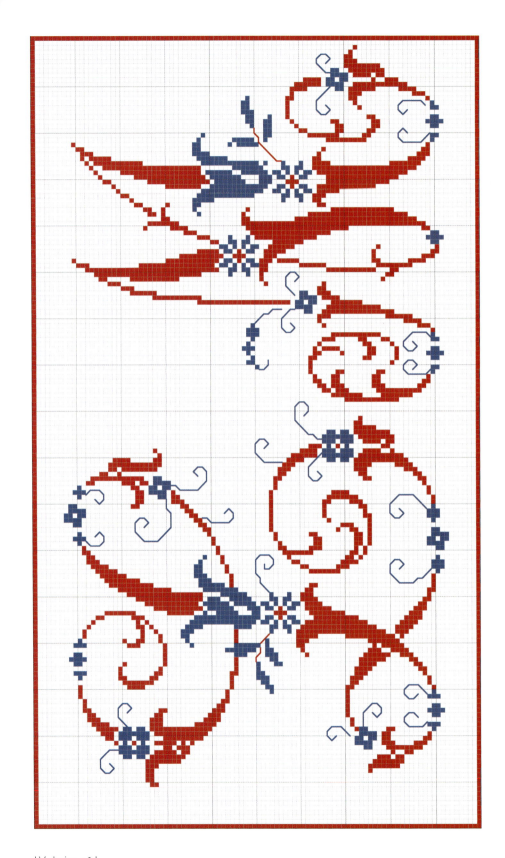

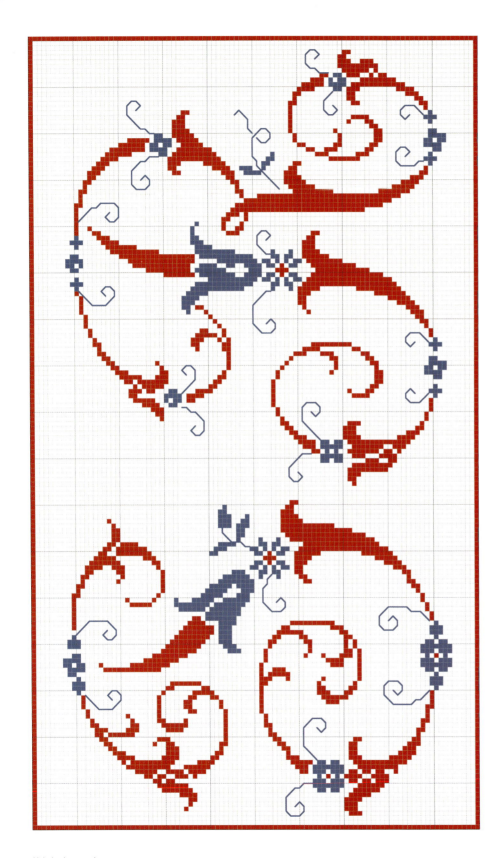

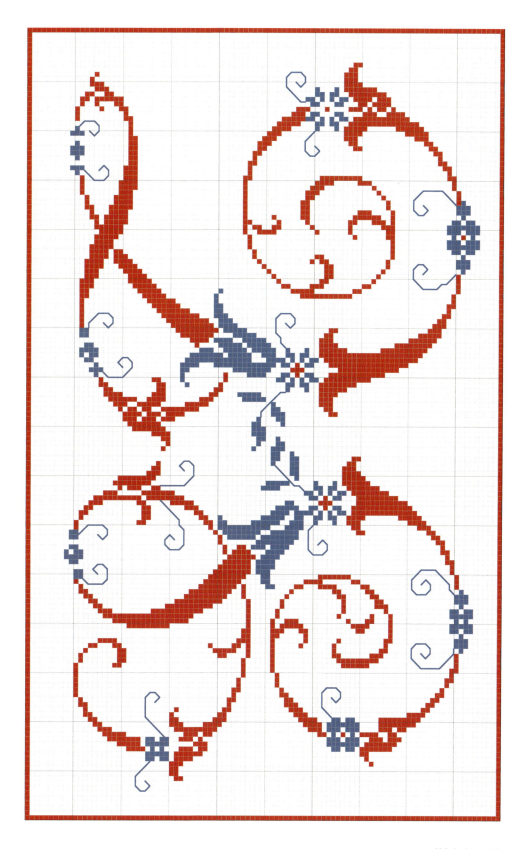

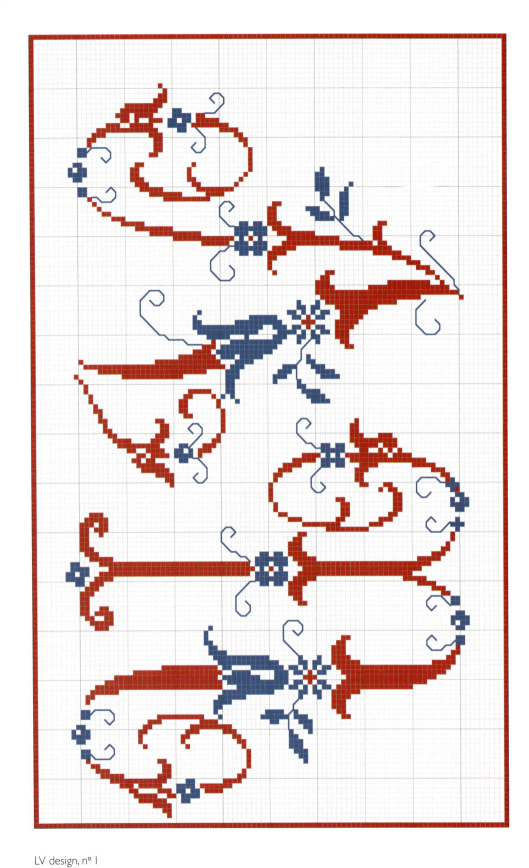

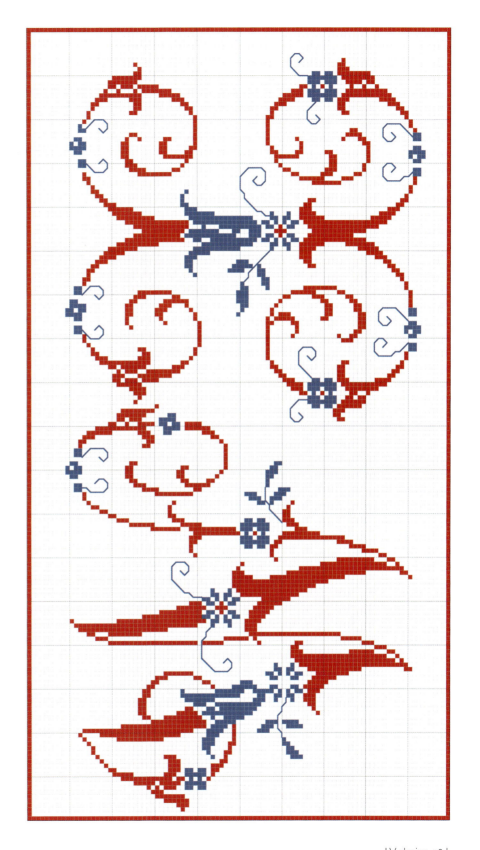

257

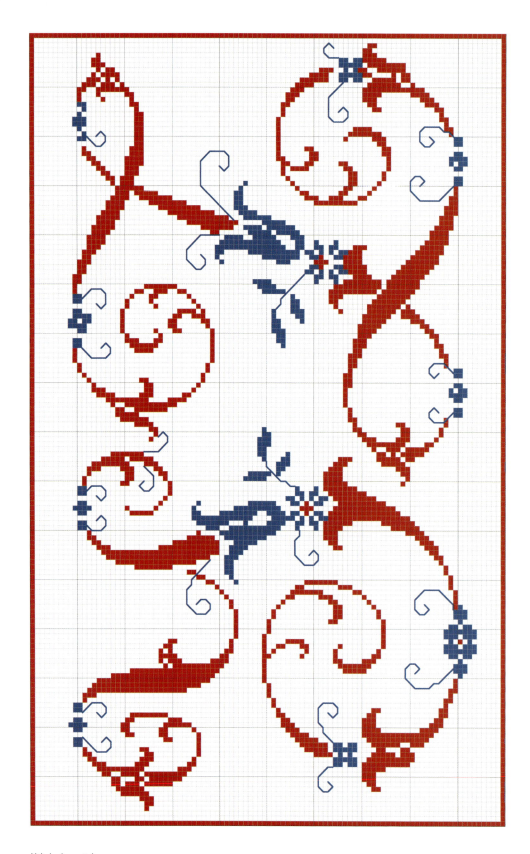

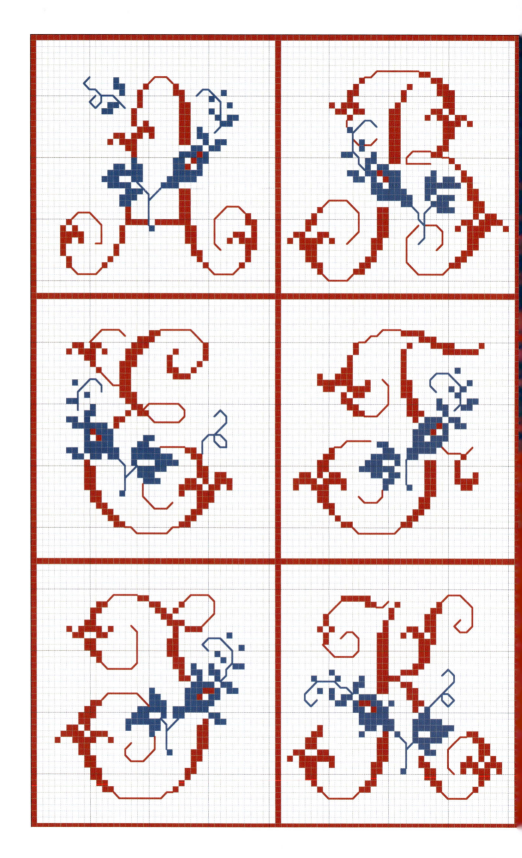

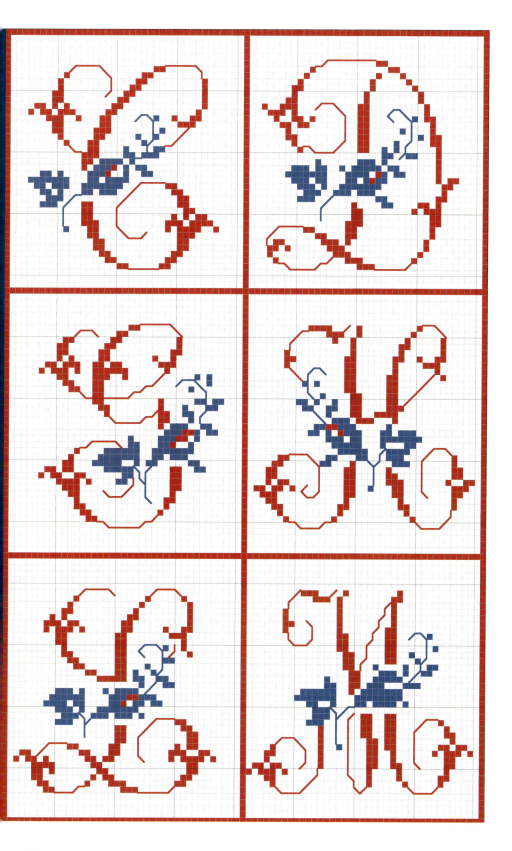

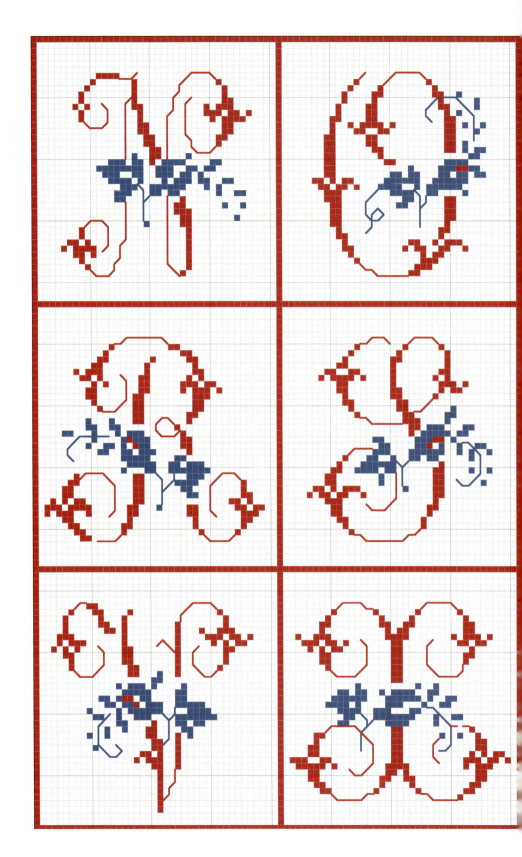

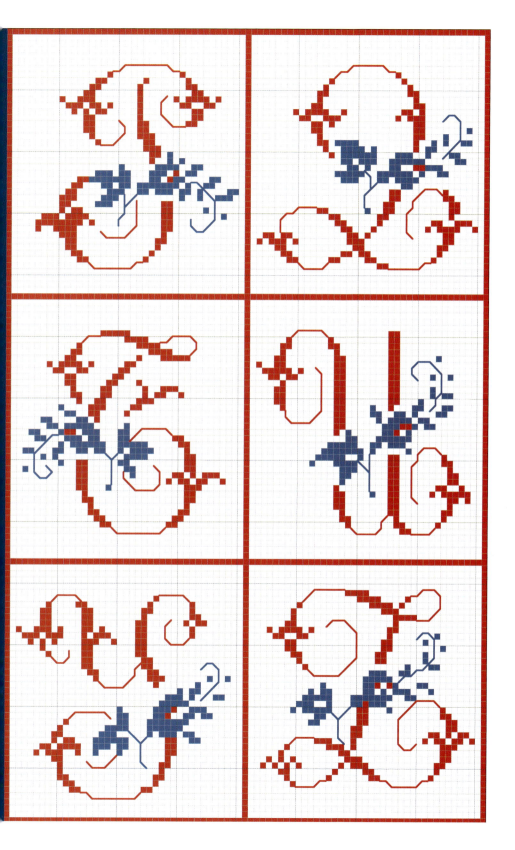

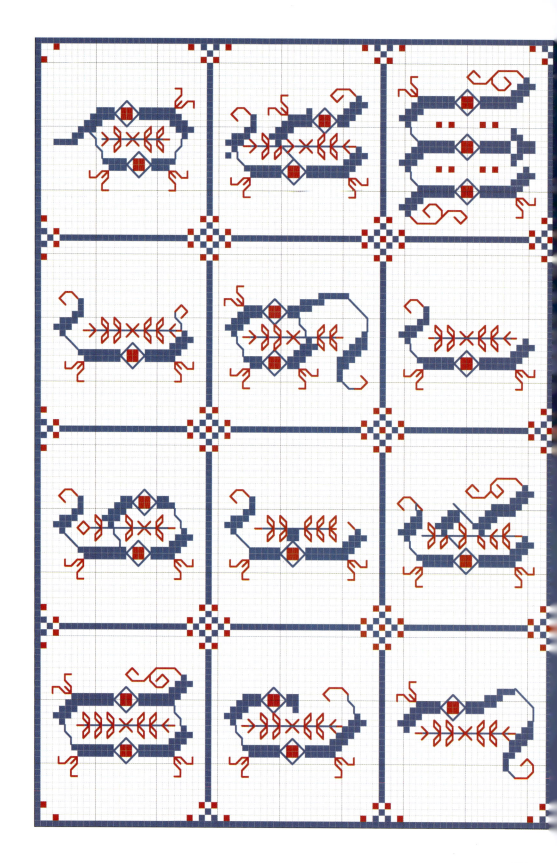

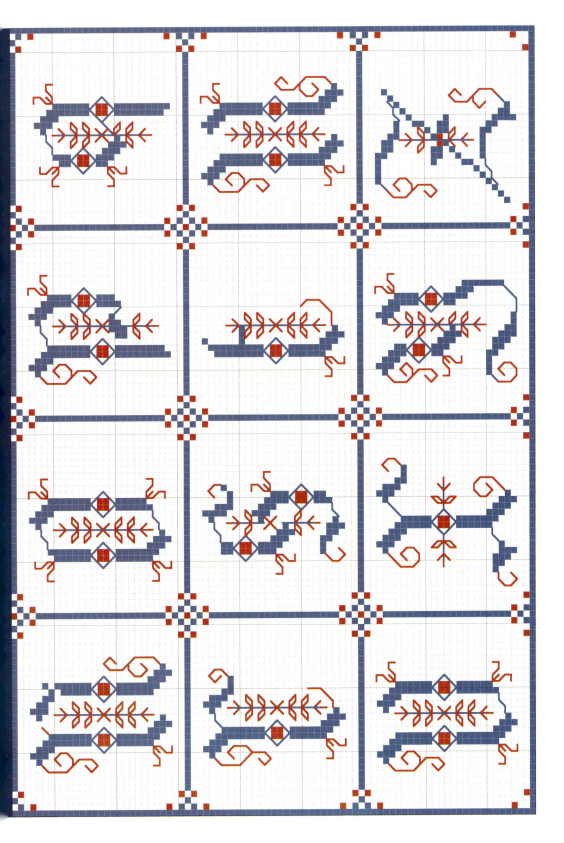

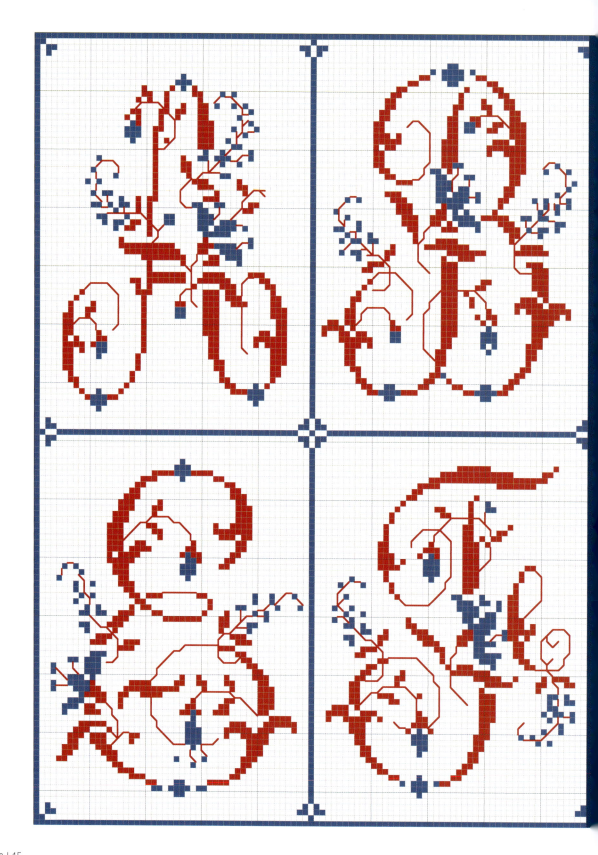

A. Rouyer, n° 145

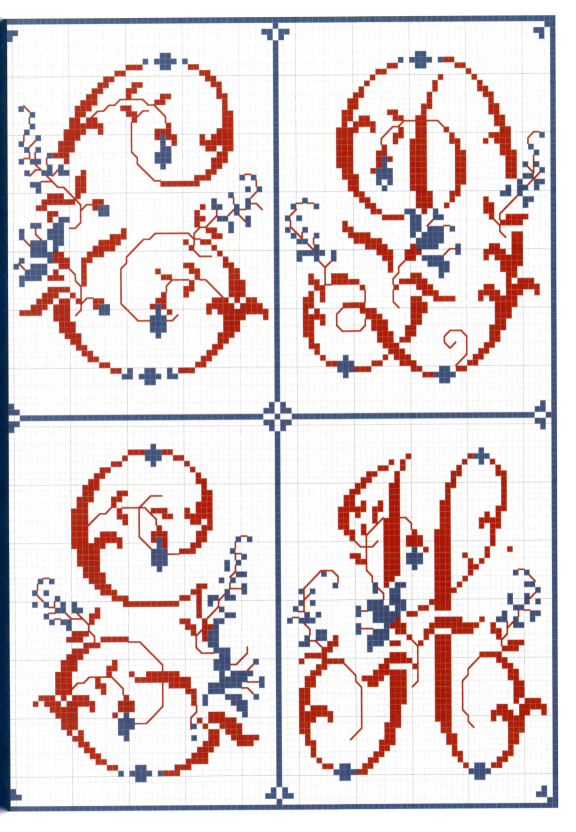

267

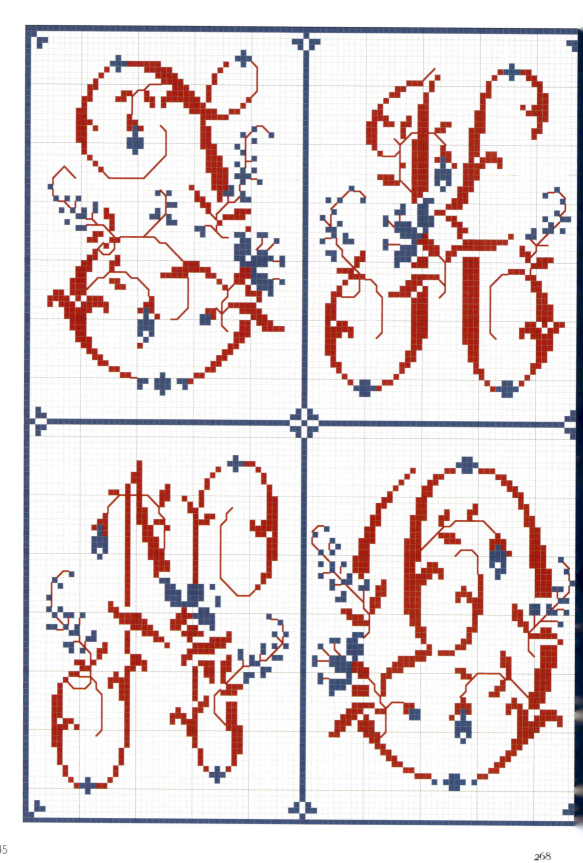

A. Rouyer, n° 145

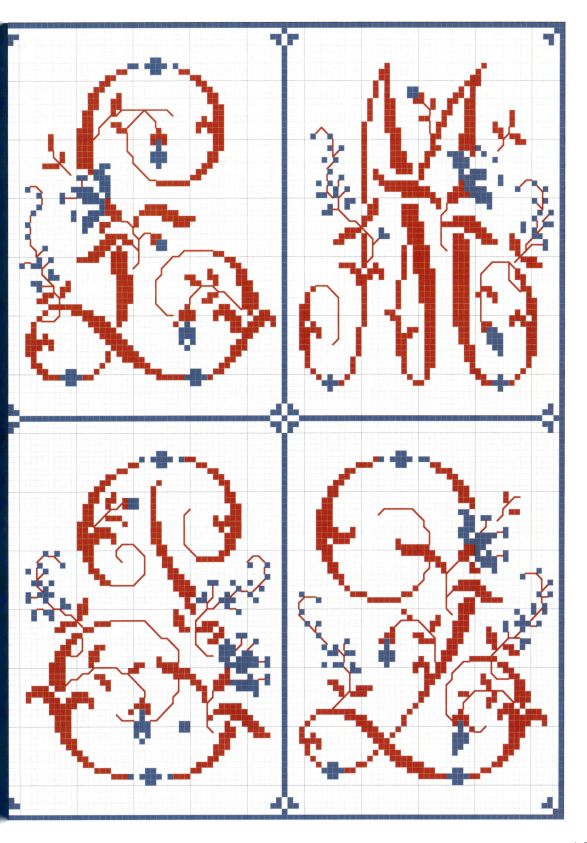

269

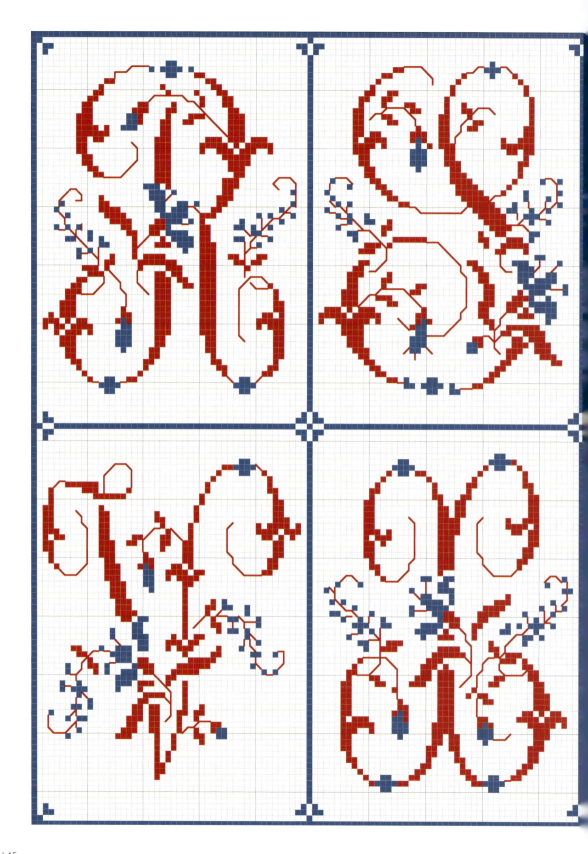

A. Rouyer, n° 145

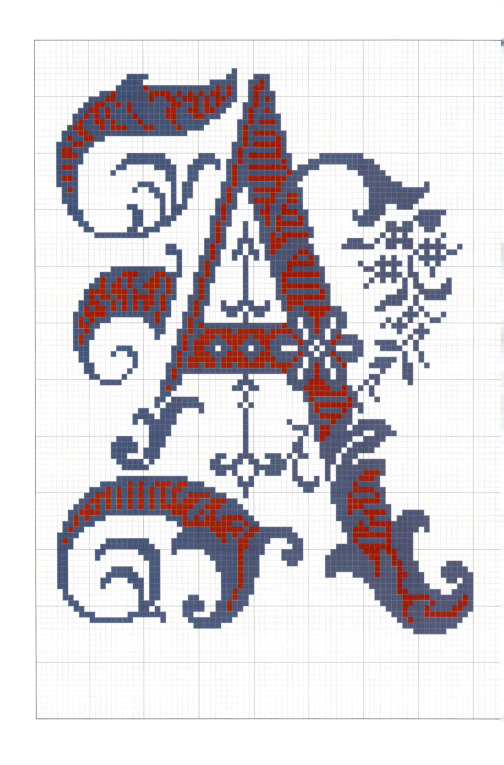

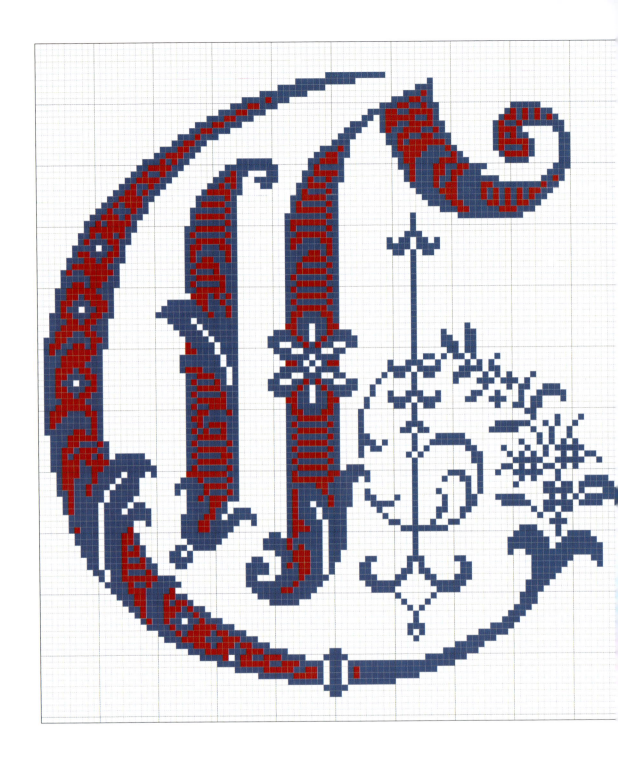

277

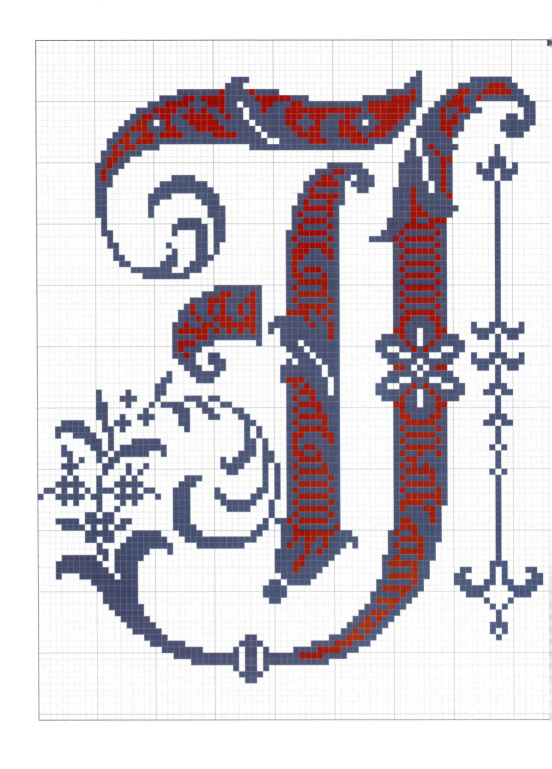

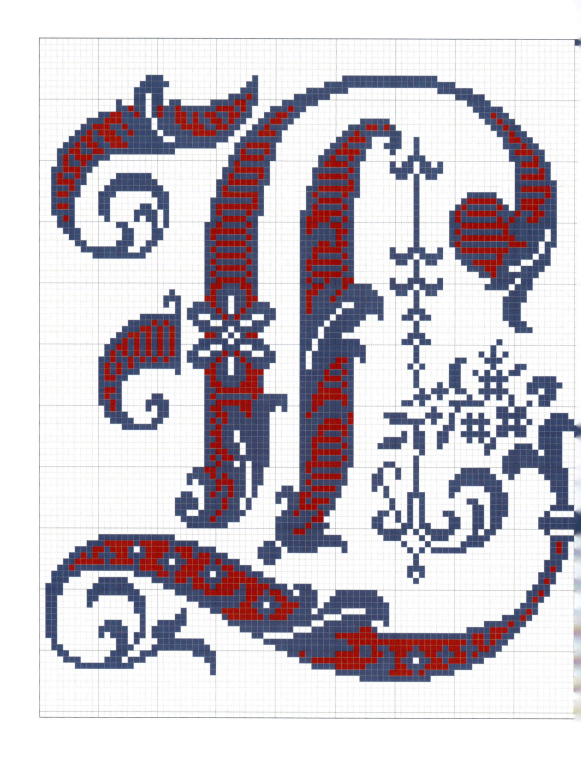

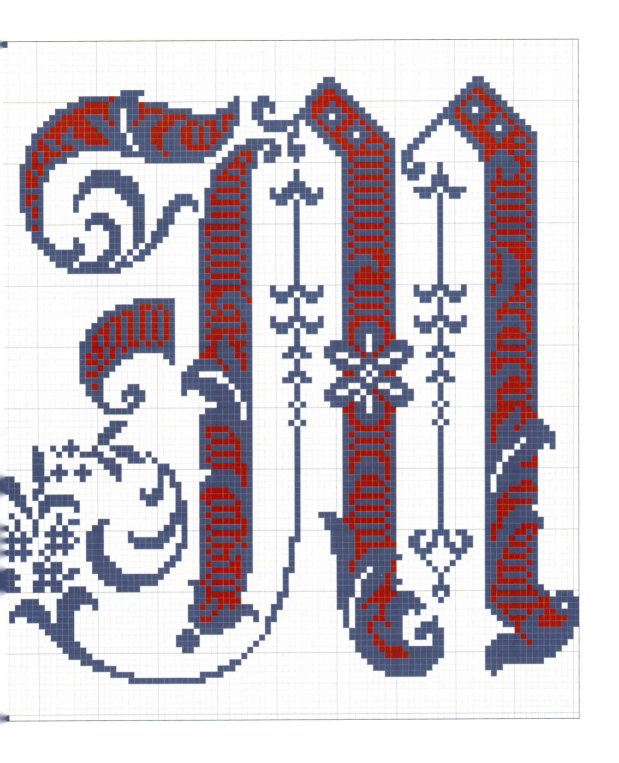

283

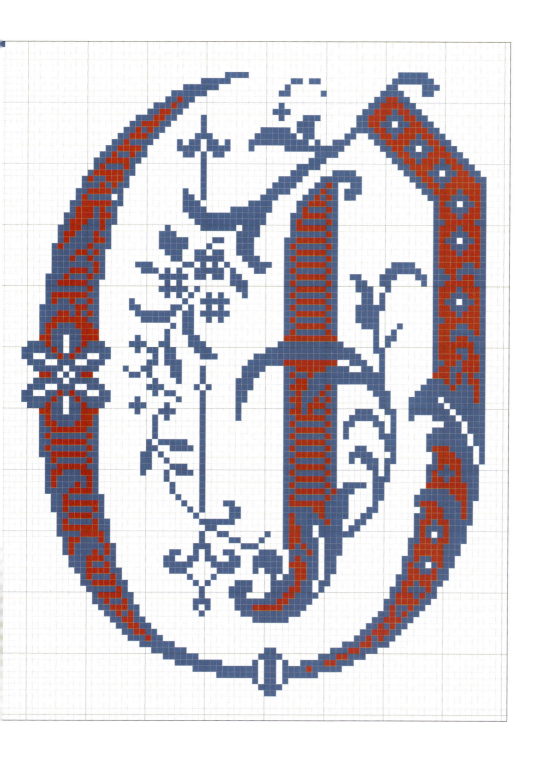

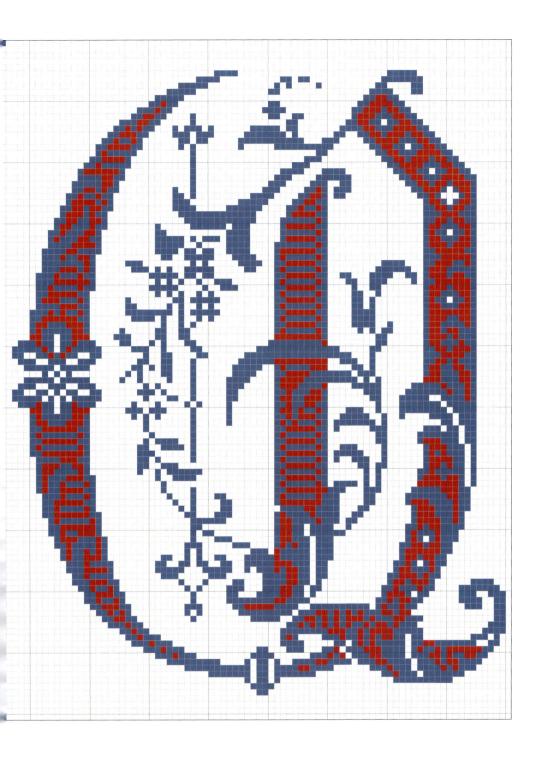

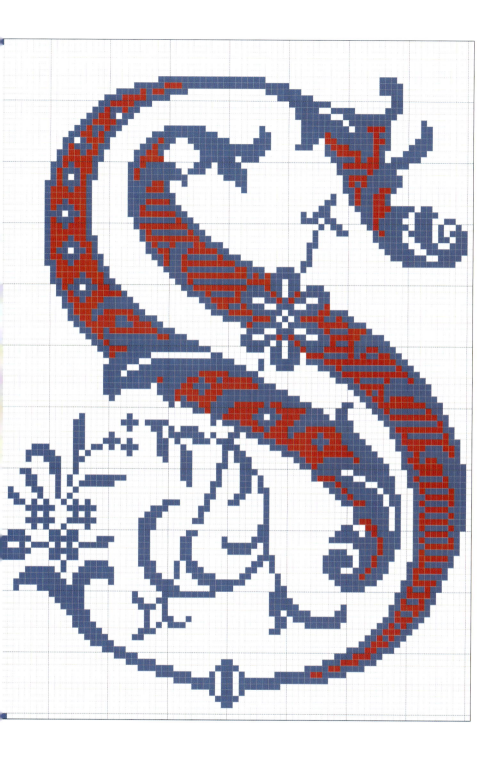

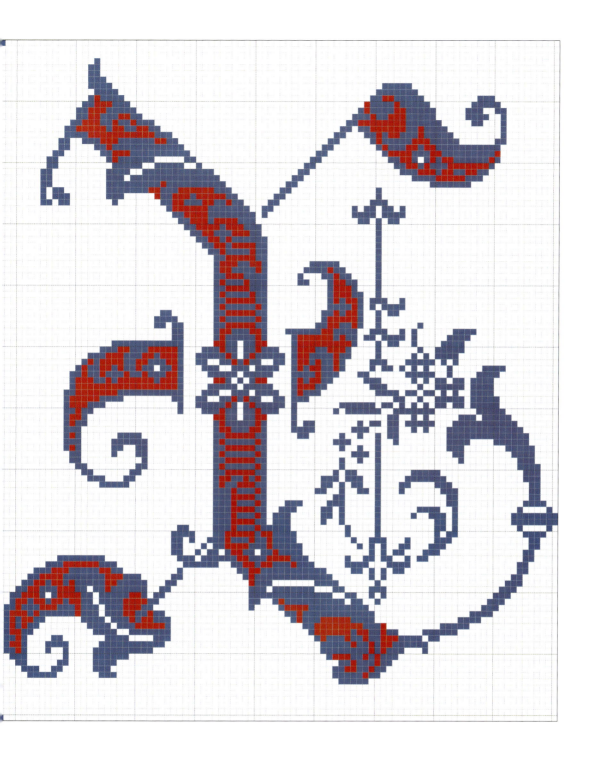

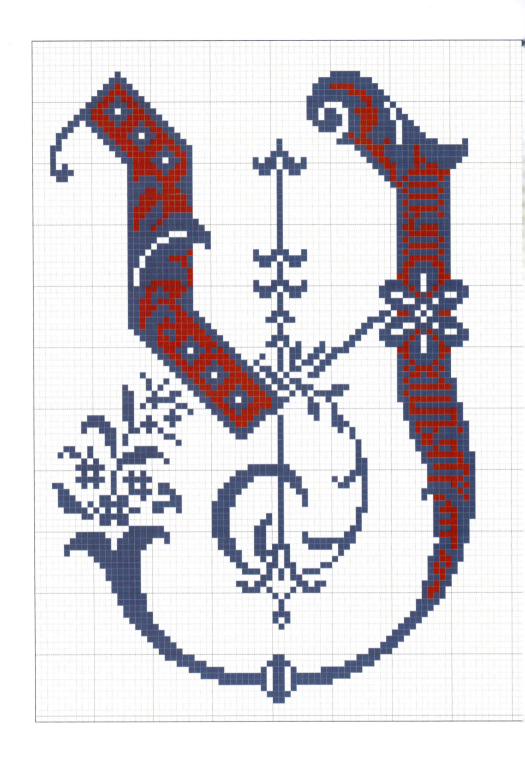

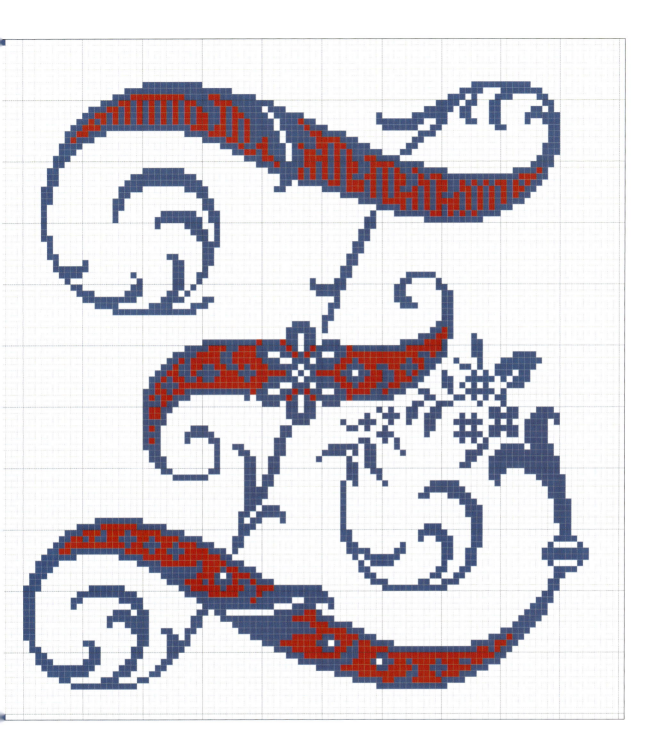

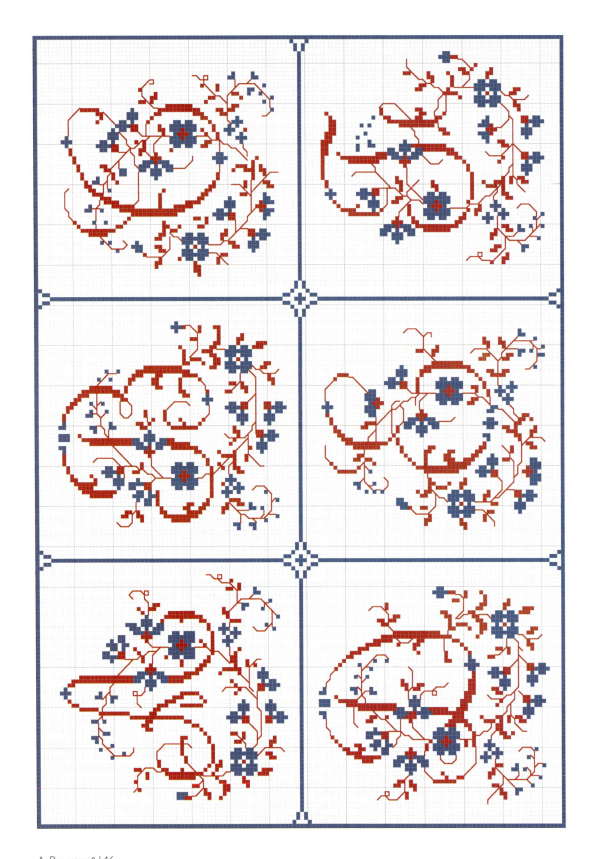

297

A. Rouyer, n° 293

A. Rouyer, nº 292

307

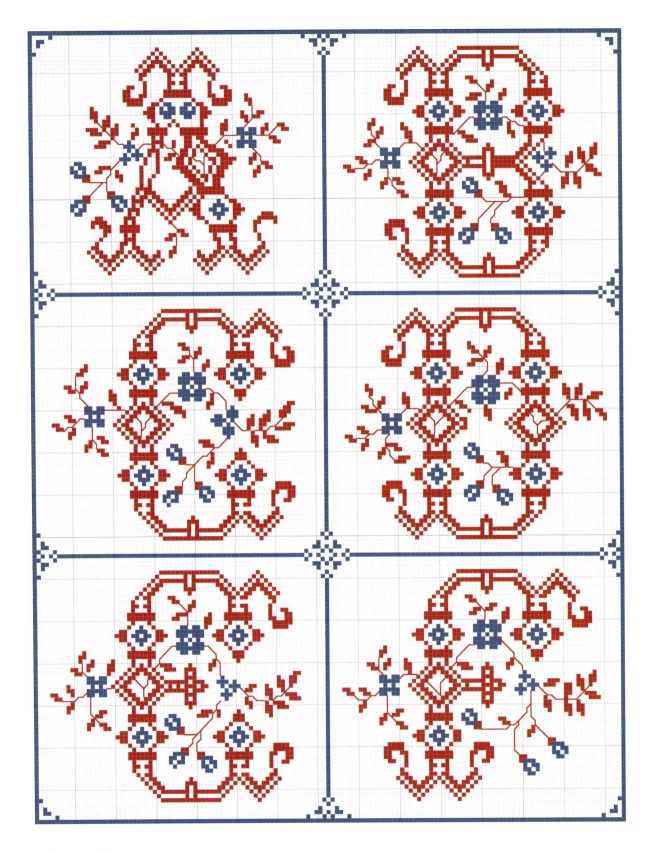

311

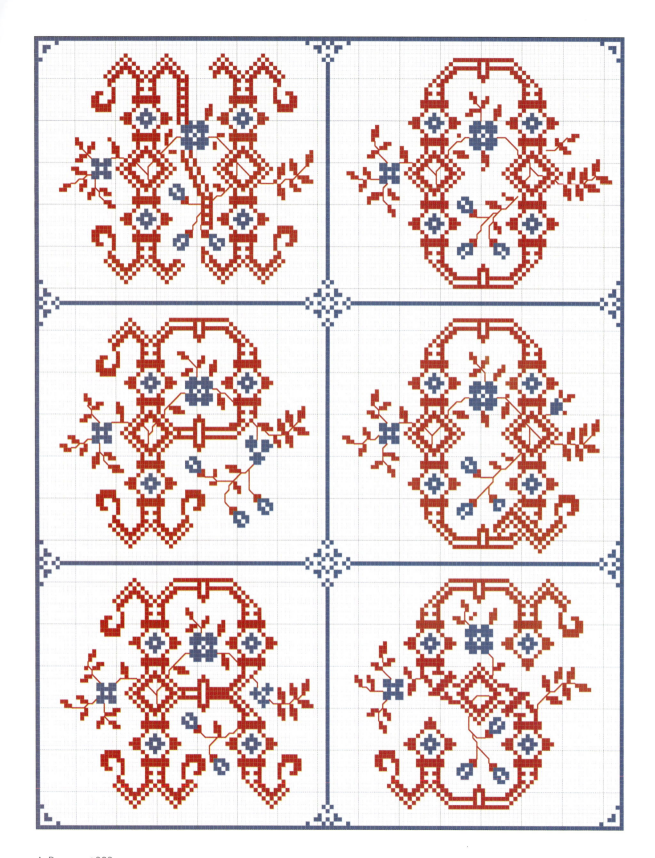

A. Rouyer, nº 293

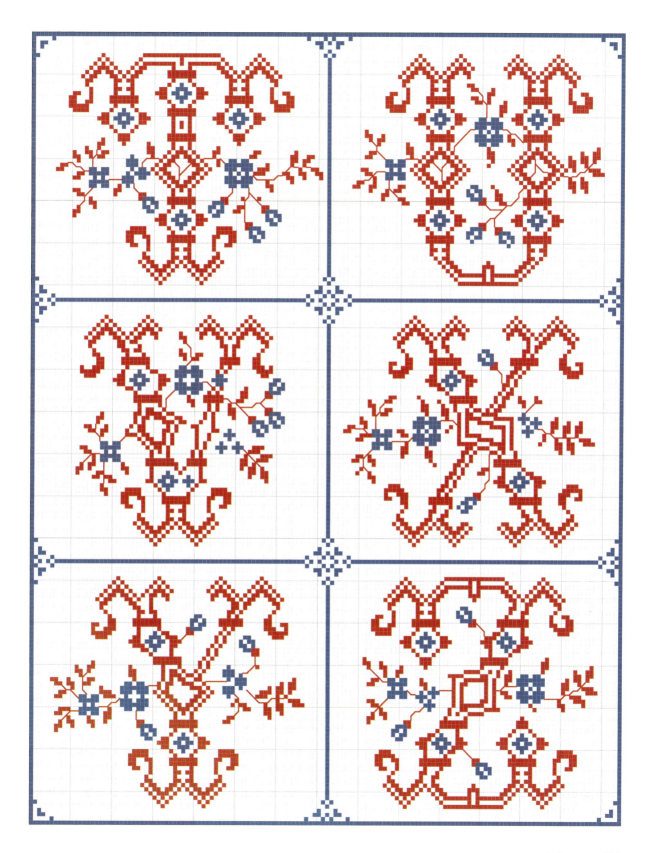

My own composition using borders and designs from Sajou, n° 186 and n° 185.
The "C" is taken from the A. Rouyer alphabet, n° 146.

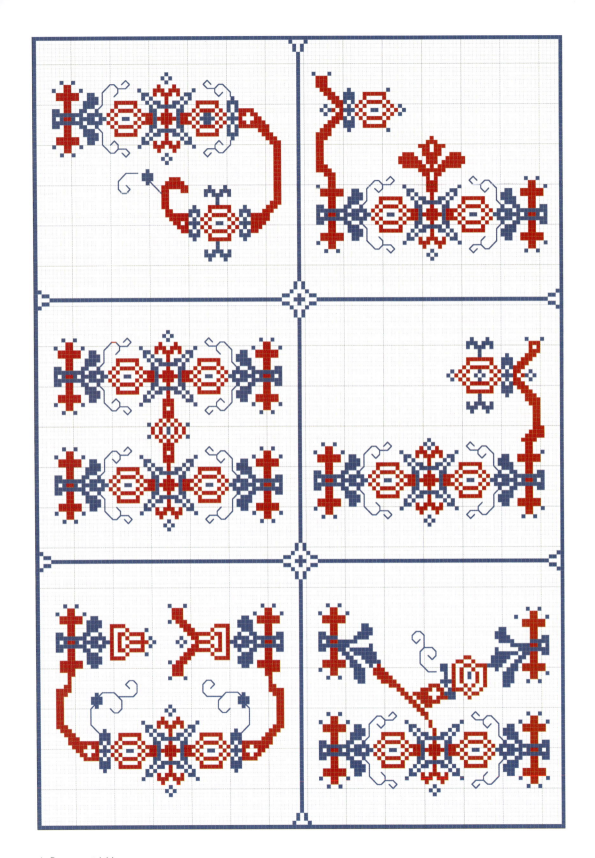

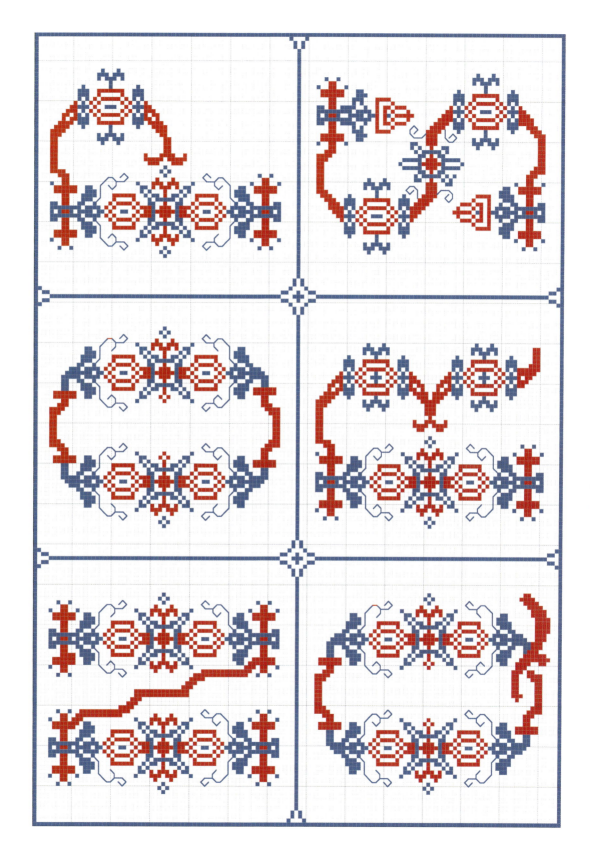

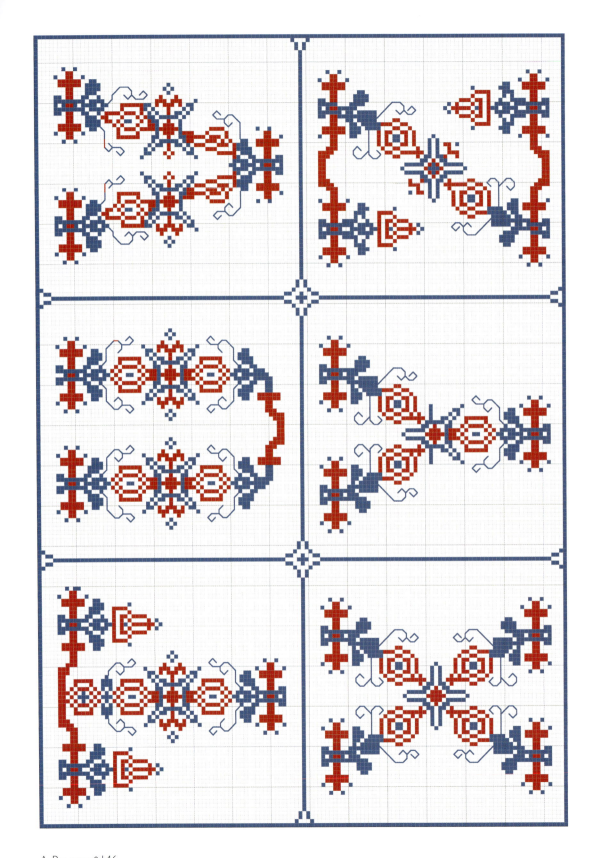

321

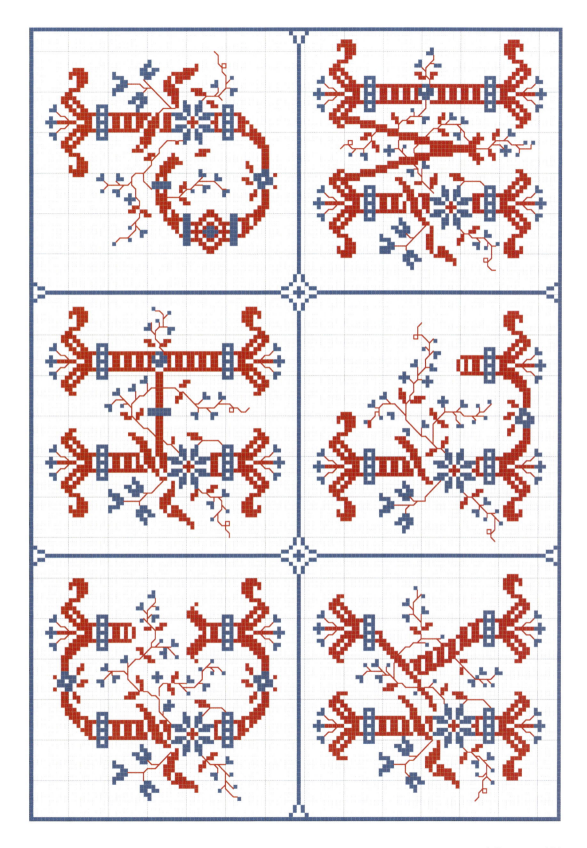

A. Rouyer, n° 144

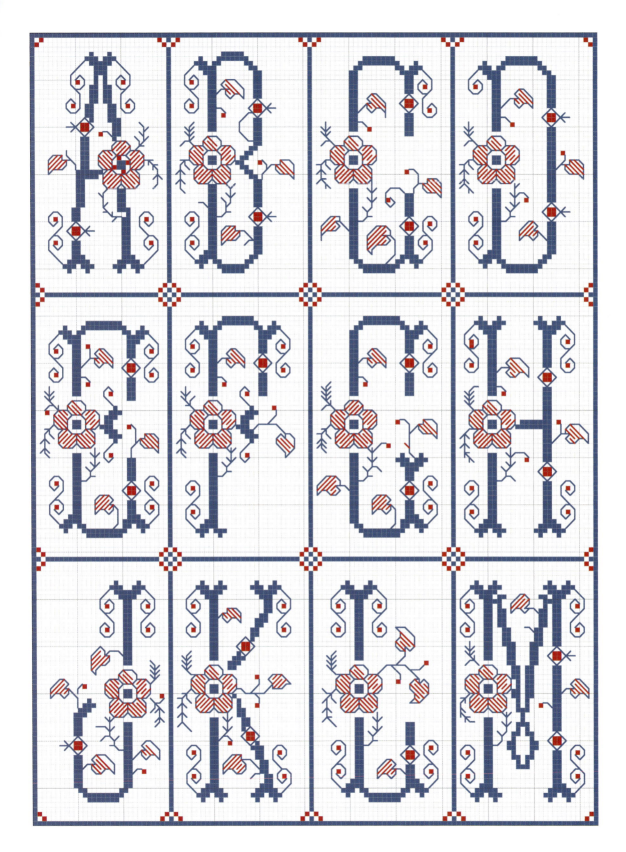

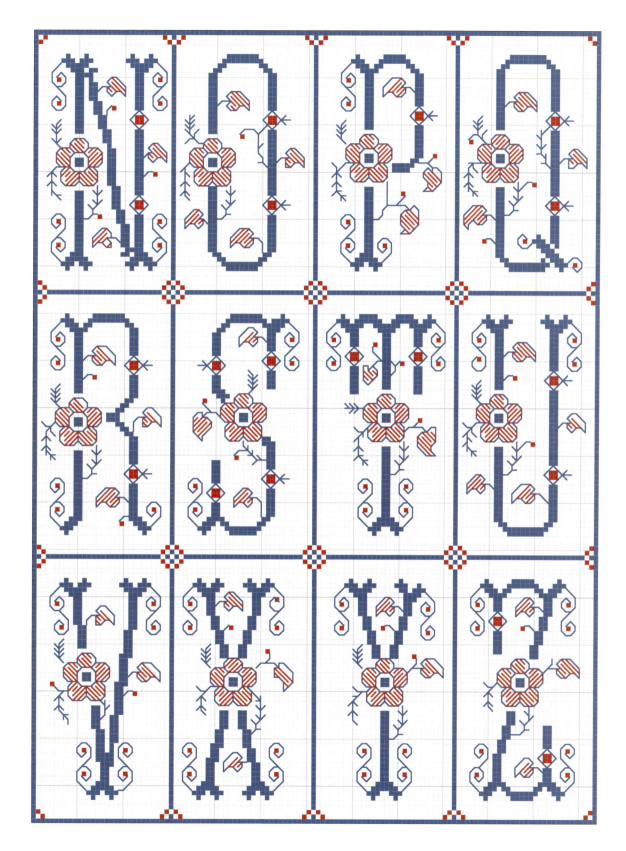

327

A. Rouyer, nº 144

A. Rouyer, n° 144

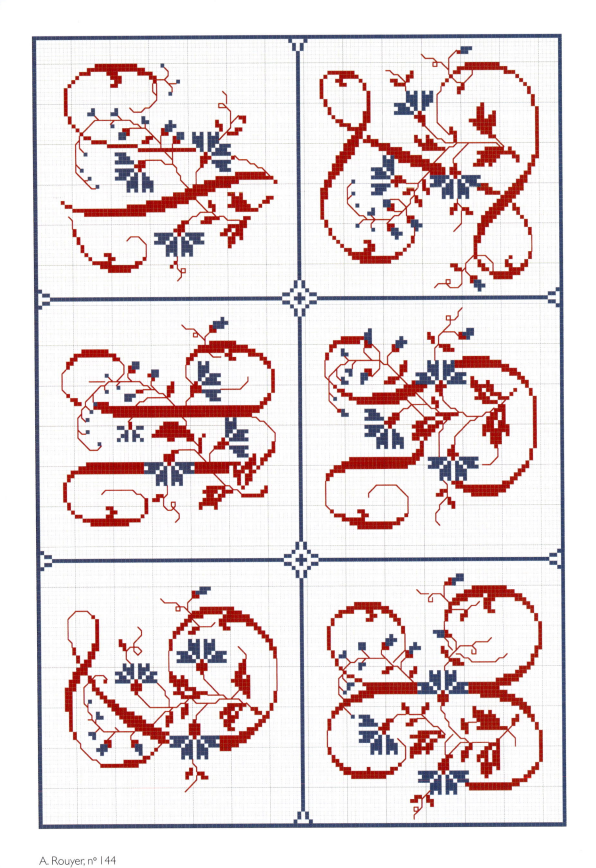

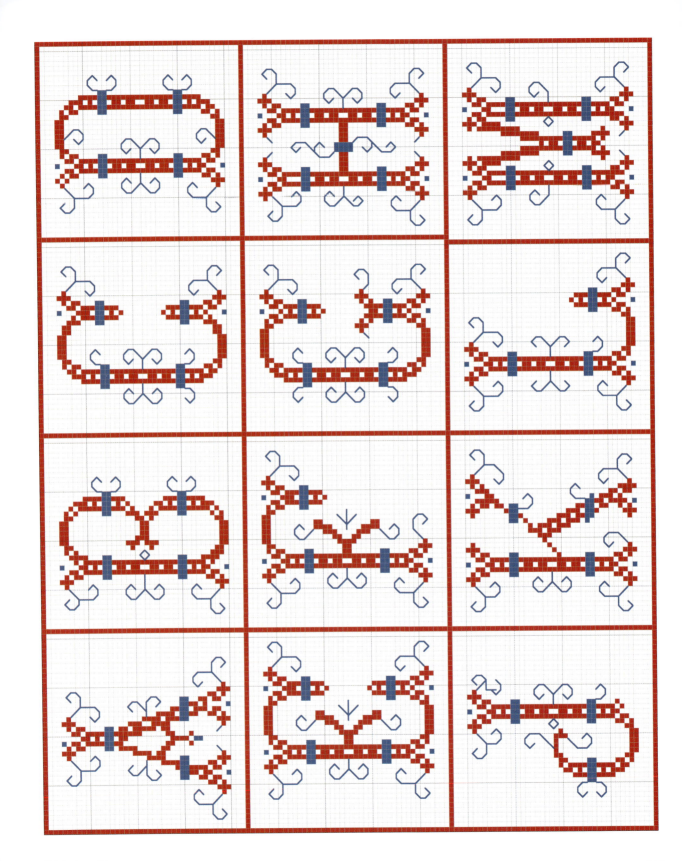

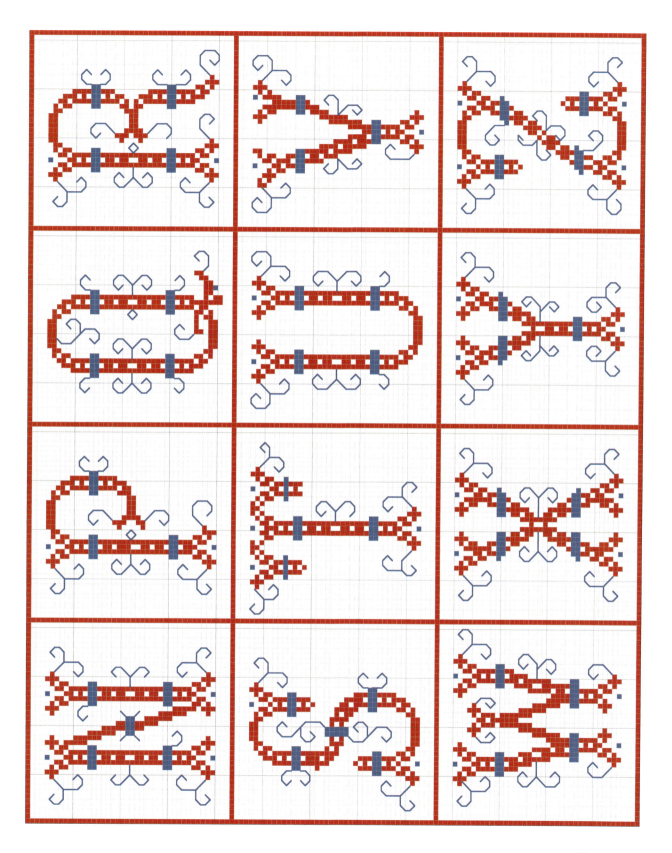

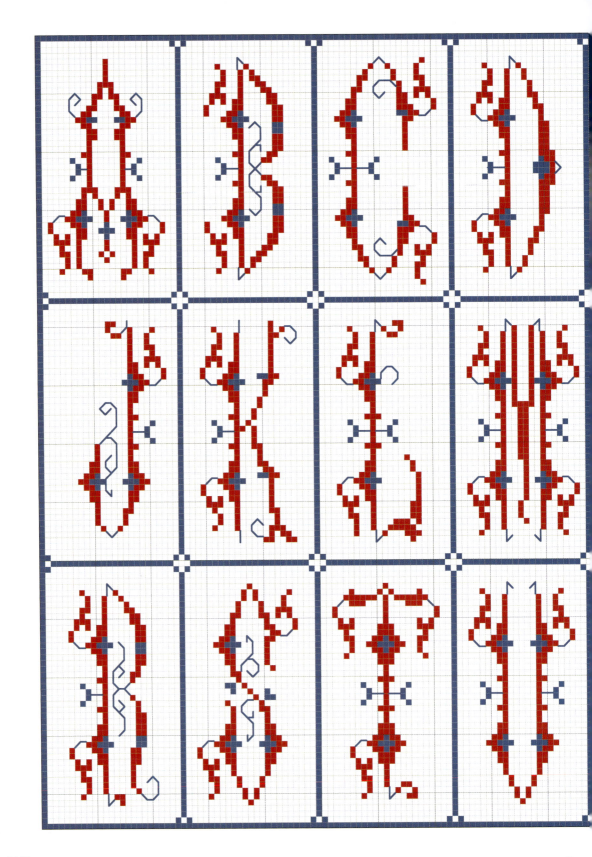

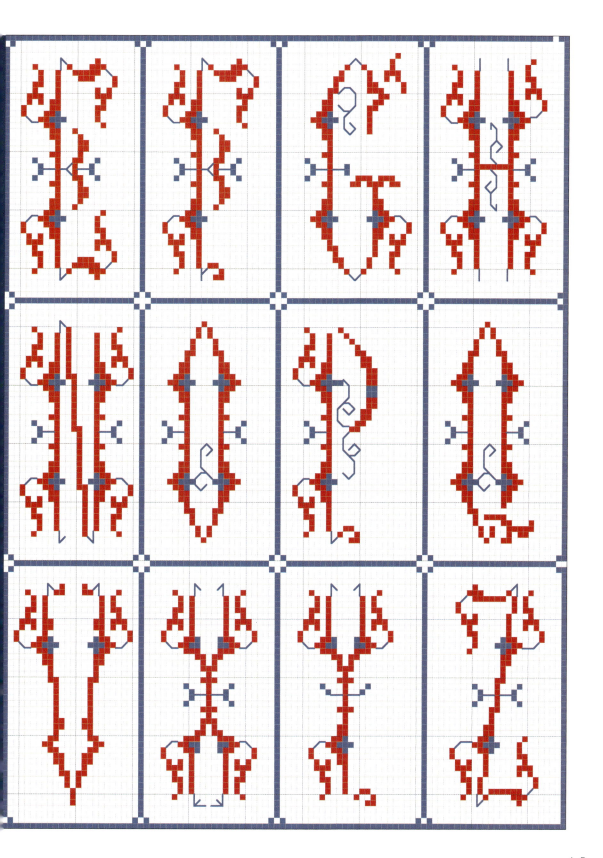

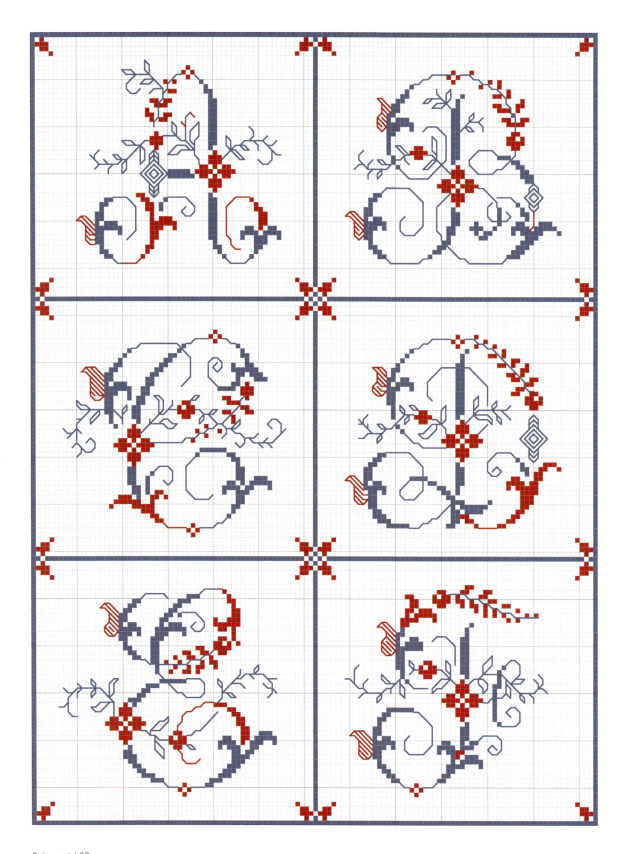

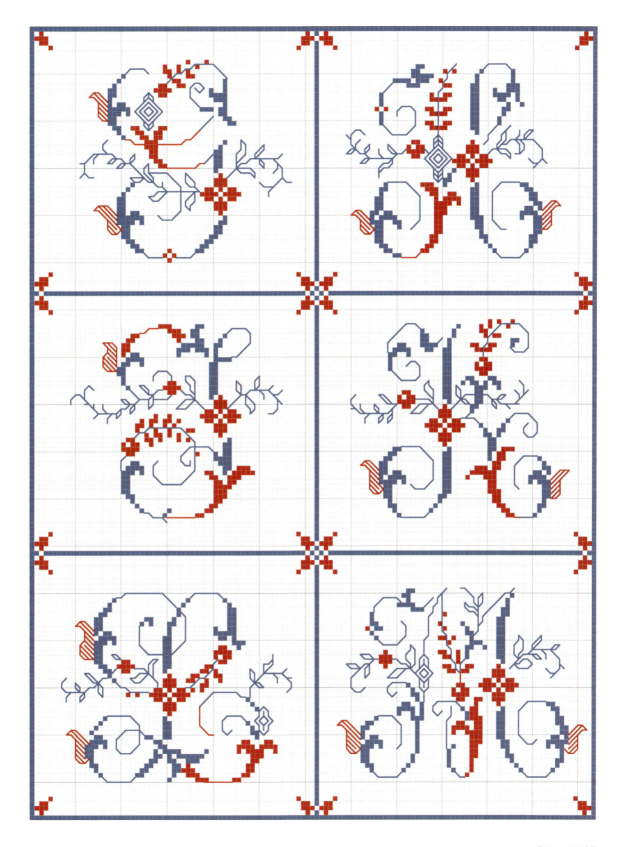

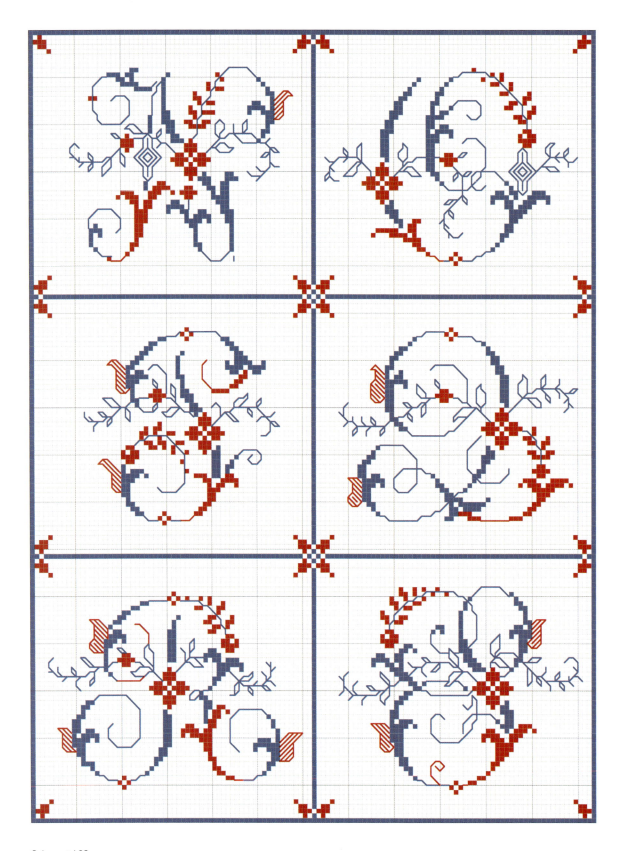

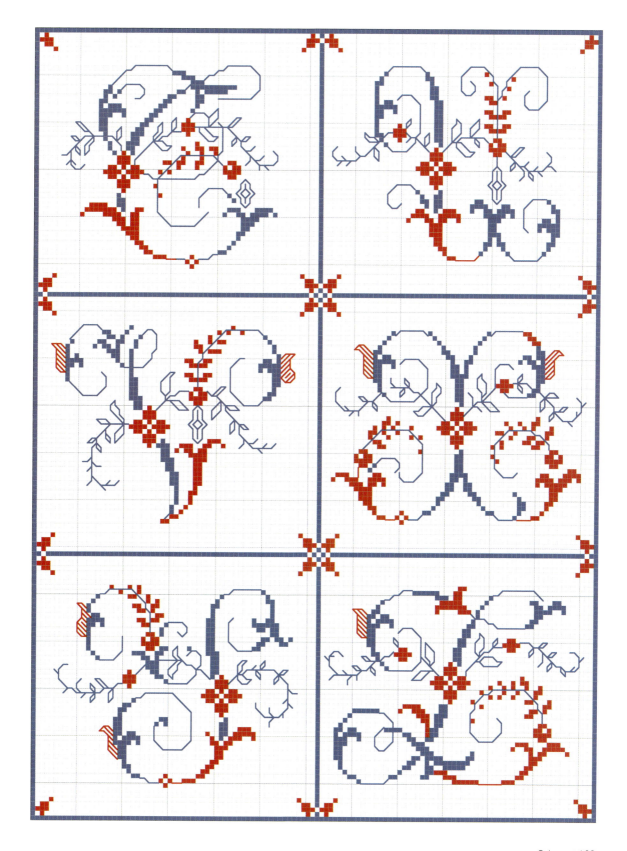

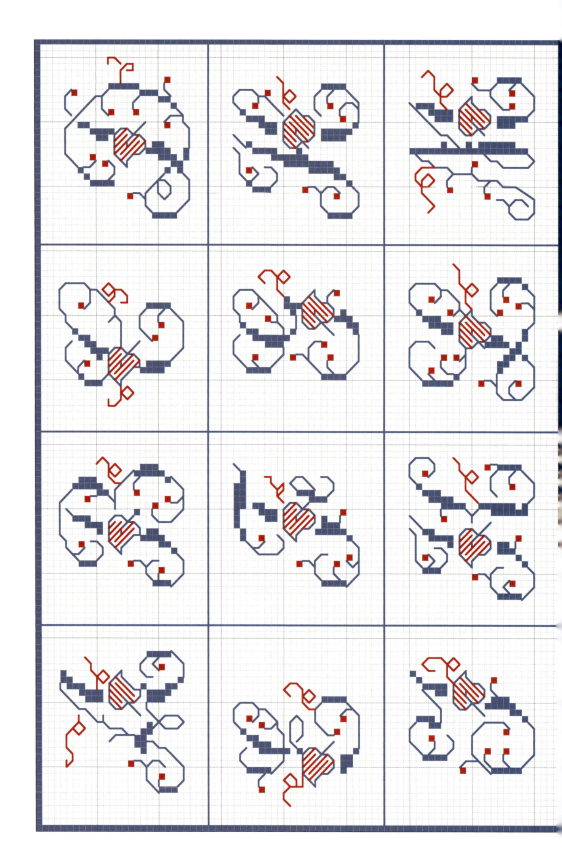

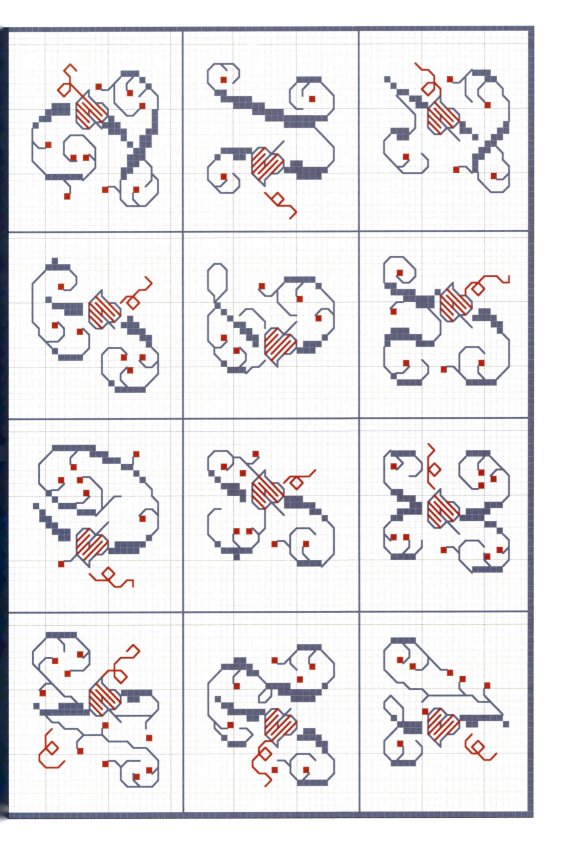

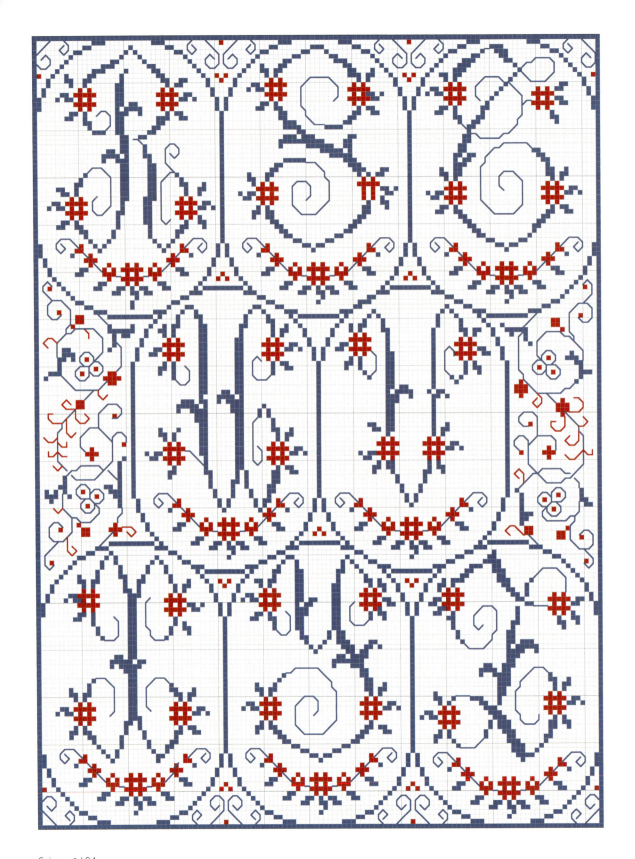

351

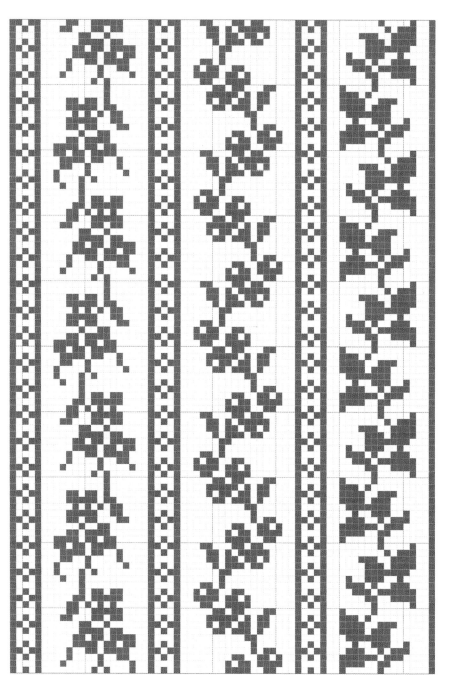

353

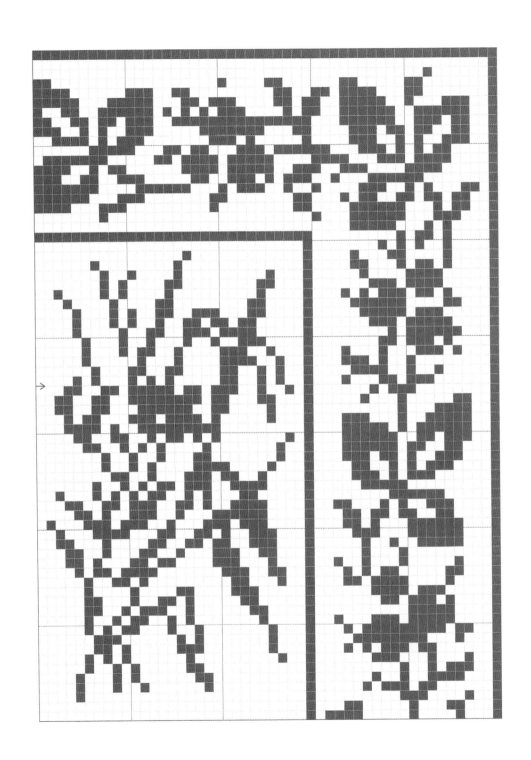

Floral motifs gleaned from various vintage pattern books.

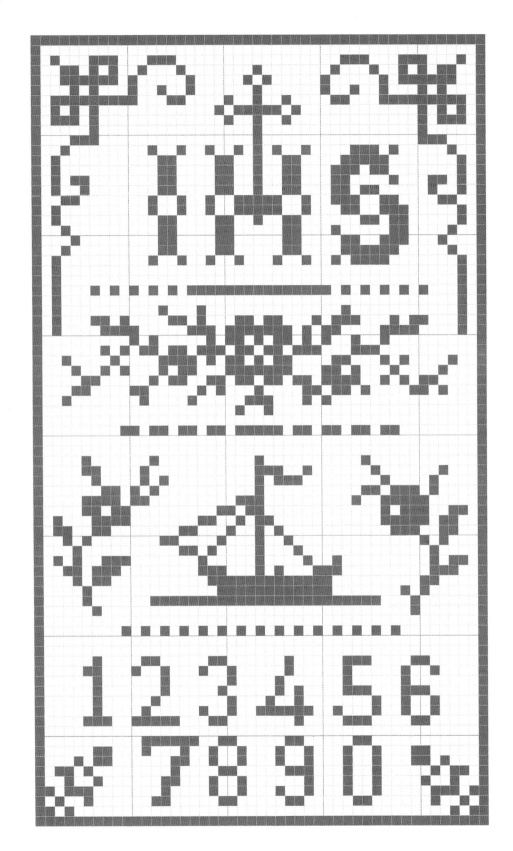

363

Sajou, n° 28 (a quarter of the motif pictured on the following page)

Entire motif

367

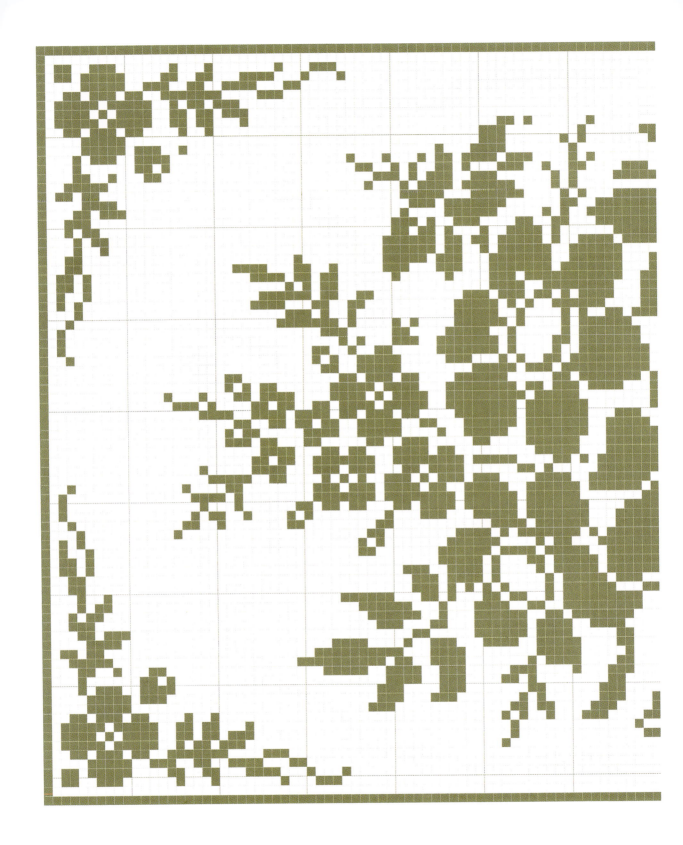

Asimart design

Asimart design

375

At the top: LV design; at the bottom: Sajou, n° 456

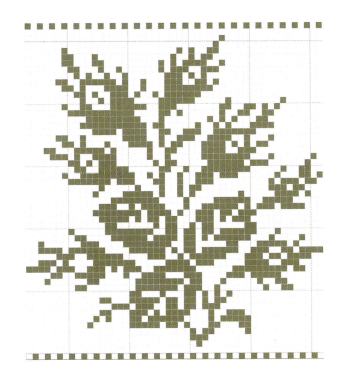

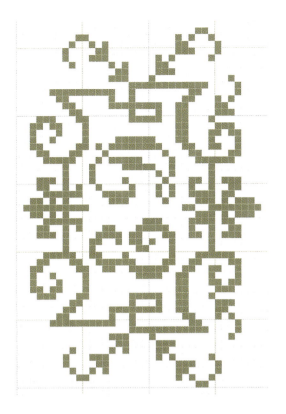

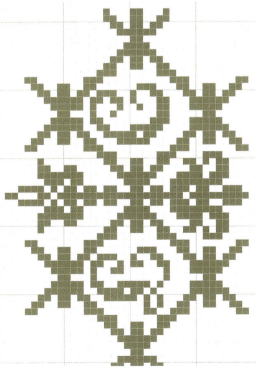

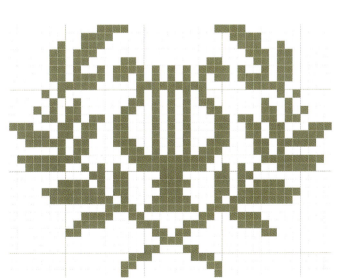

379

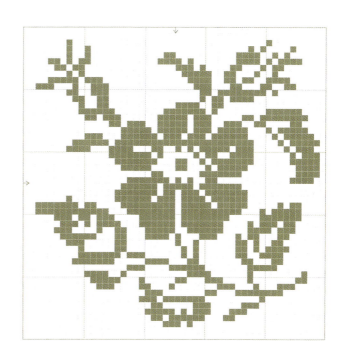

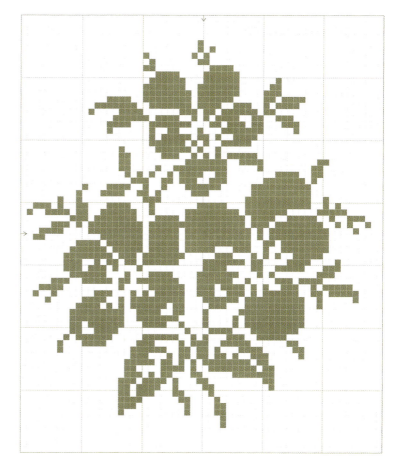

Unknown author

387

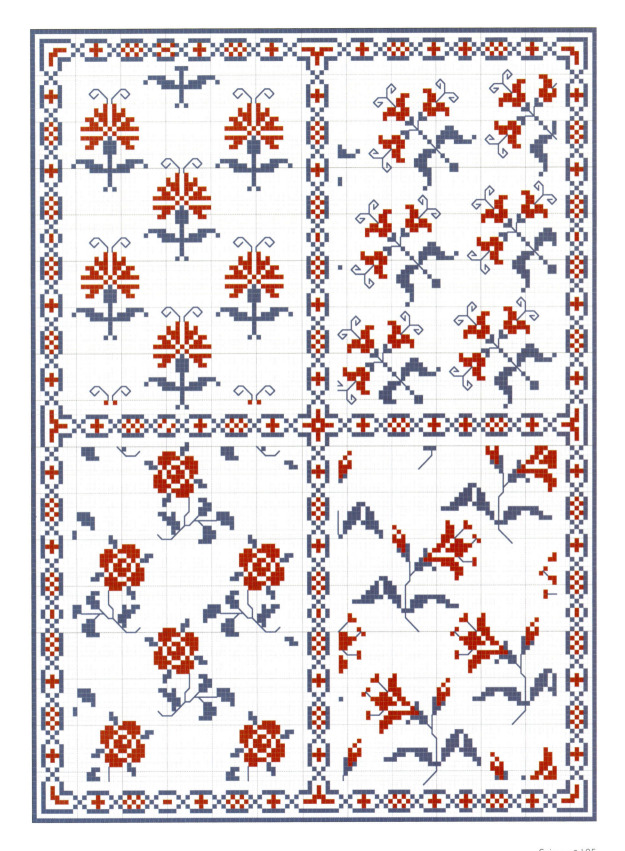

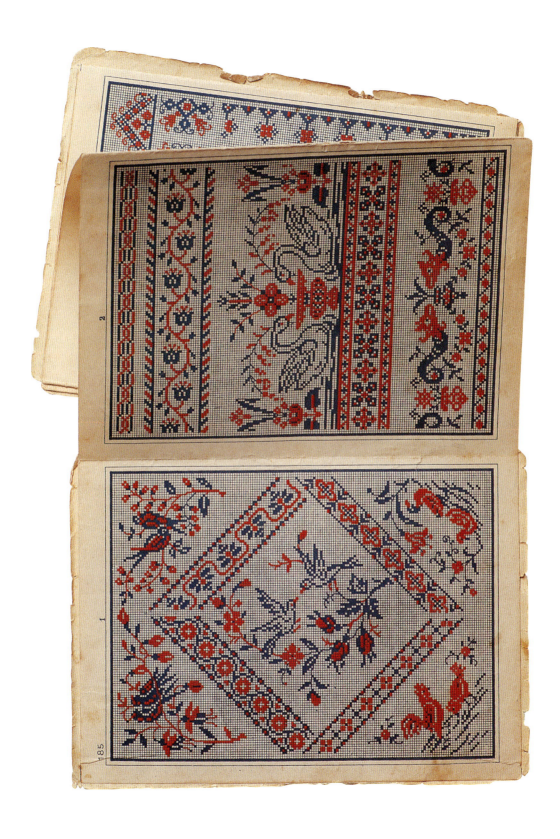

Egg warmers, embroidered using Sajou, n° 186, and Sajou, n° 185;
napkin holders designed using the border in Sajou, n° 186.

401

Design from Berlin

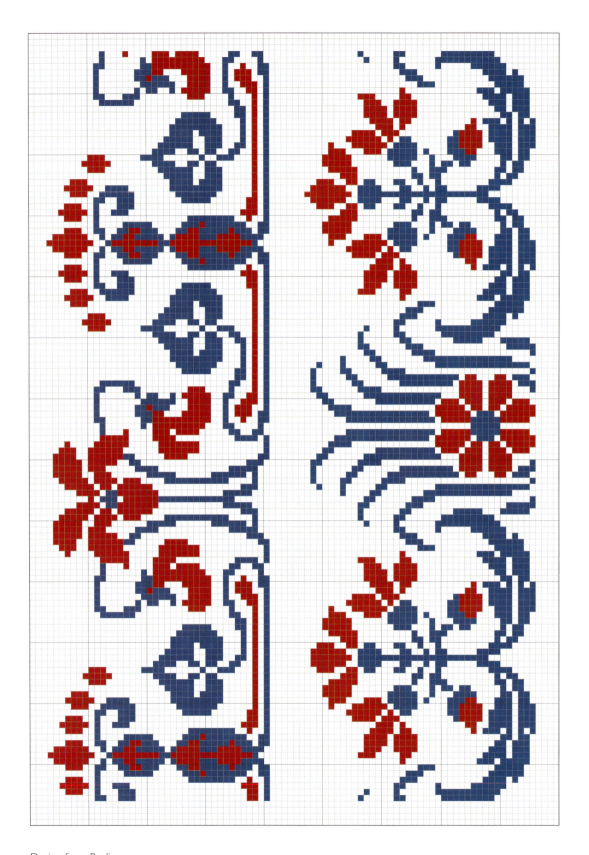

Design from Berlin

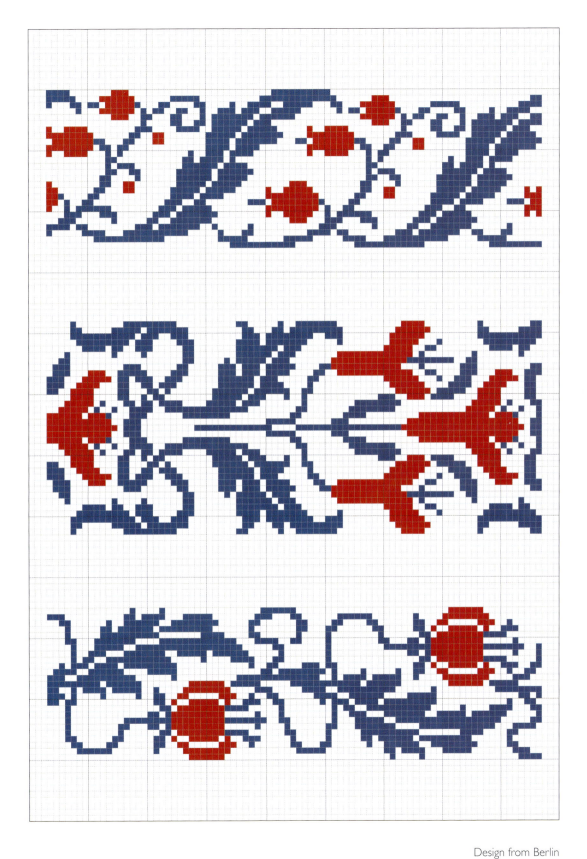

Design from Berlin

Design from Berlin

407

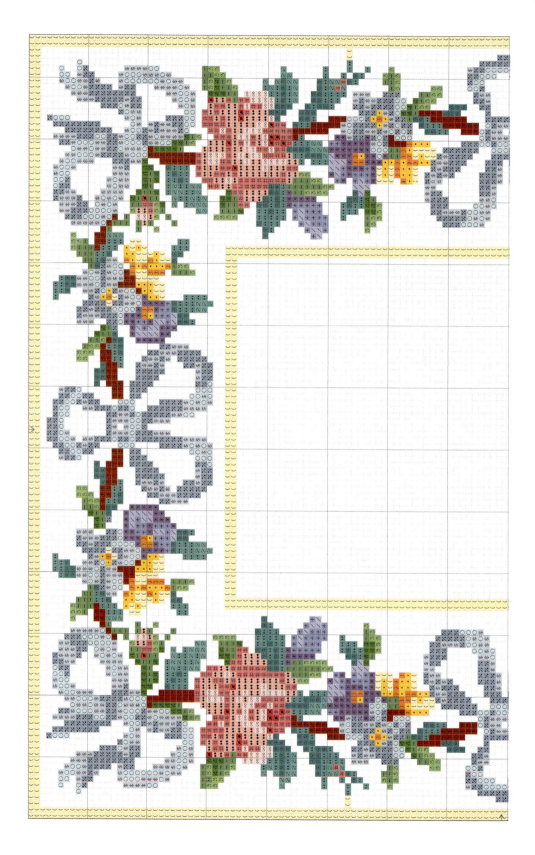

◇◇	225
◆◆	224
#	223
∮	3721
/	341
+	340
*	3746
O	3752
$	932
%	931
3	3348
—	3347
4	3346
2	503
••	502
o	501
(	744
•	743
)	977
↑	433

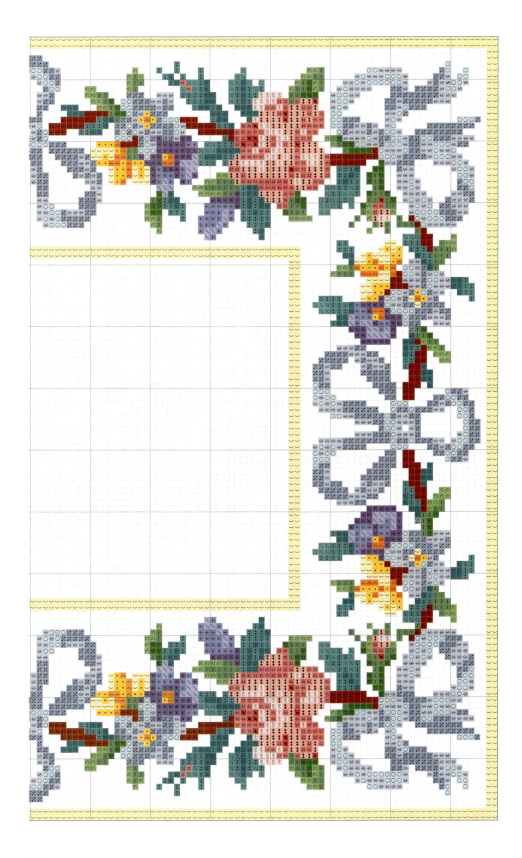

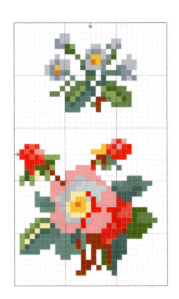

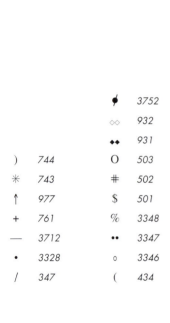

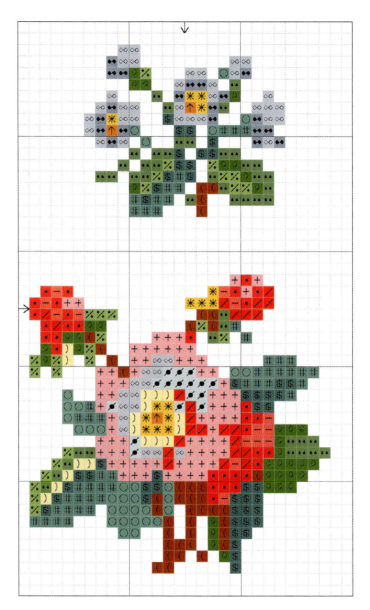

		◆	3752
		⬦⬦	932
		◆◆	931
)	744	O	503
✳	743	#	502
↑	977	$	501
+	761	%	3348
—	3712	••	3347
•	3328	○	3346
/	347	(	434

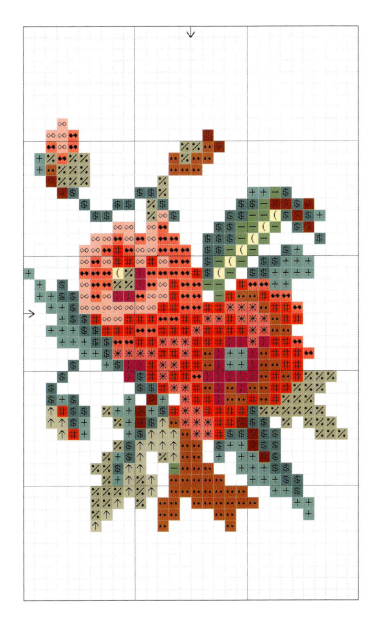

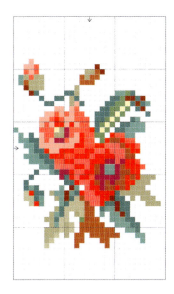

✳	3712
⧖	353
◆◆	351
♯	349
)	3685
+	503
$	501
↑	3013
%	3012
—	3347
••	435
○	433
(	744

(	300
○	301
✳	319
#	320
☆	367
$	402
—	503
◇◇	610
)	613
••	743
%	745
■	918
•	921
✳	986
+	987
↑	989

2	white	#	498			
/	3041	O	646	◇◇	814	
••	309	✦	648	◆◆	815	
4	319	+	720	3	898	
$	321	↑	721	o	899	
8	3348	✳	722	—	902	
✚	367	)	744	6	988	
•	3721	(	776	7	989	

A. Rouyer, n° 352

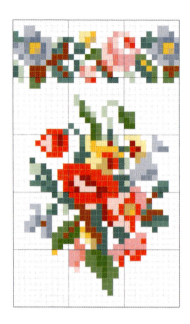

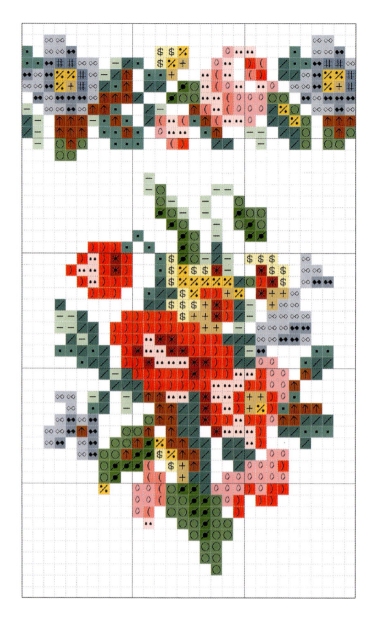

✳	3777	◇◇	932
+	834	◆◆	931
↑	434	#	930
—	504	$	744
•	502	%	743
/	501	••	3713
O	3347	o	761
✦	3346	(	760
		)	350

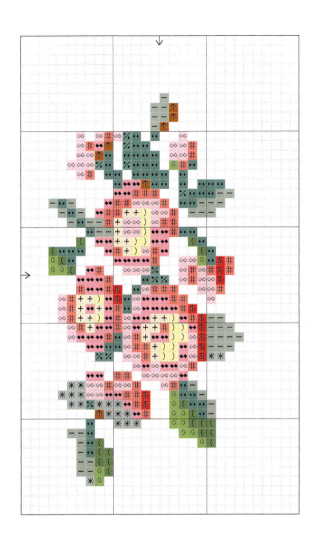

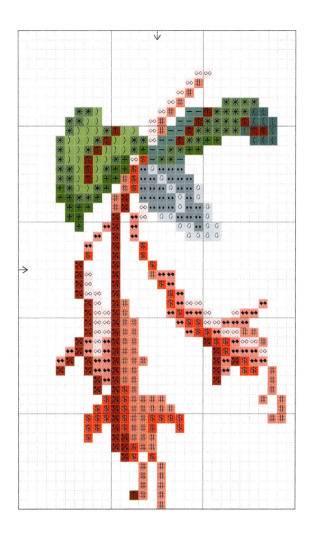

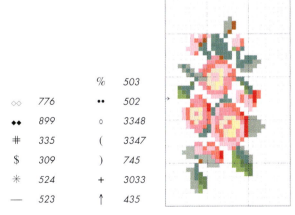

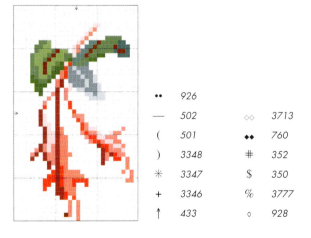

			%	503
◇◇	776		••	502
◆◆	899		o	3348
#	335		(	3347
$	309		)	745
✳	524		+	3033
—	523		↑	435

••	926			
—	502		◇◇	3713
(	501		◆◆	760
)	3348		#	352
✳	3347		$	350
+	3346		%	3777
↑	433		o	928

A. Rouyer, n° 177

••	3041
▼	319
)	367
%	3726
o	3743
(	3776
$	3802
#	3820
◆◆	3822
✳	503
O	745
◇◇	936
+	987
↑	989

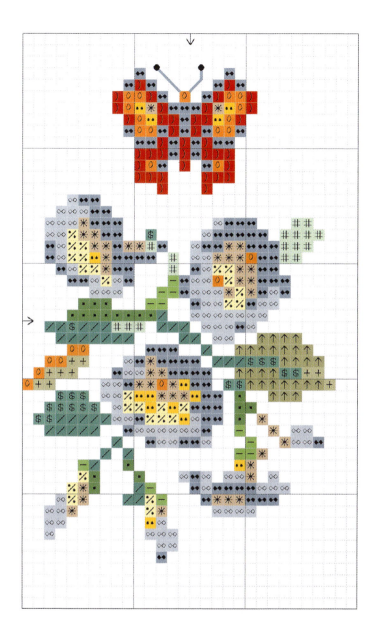

◇◇	932	○	977
◆◆	931	)	355
#	504	✳	3782
$	503	+	3013
/	502	↑	3012
%	744	—	3348
••	743	•	3347

A. Rouyer, n° 178

⊕	503	◡	987	❖	334	◯	3731	⊞	814	⌘	3033
☆	367	⊠	3752	✳	819	2	3721	6	902	⬌	3782
◇	500	†	932	♣	3326	◇◇	498	φ	743	⫲	3032
☐	989	4	930	⊥	3733	♦♦	815	♡	977	$	9999

A. Rouyer design

$	3325
%	334
◇◇	340
O	355
◗	356
+	501
↑	503
—	504
⌗	550
◆◆	553
)	744
✳	775
•	829
/	977
••	987
○	988
(	989

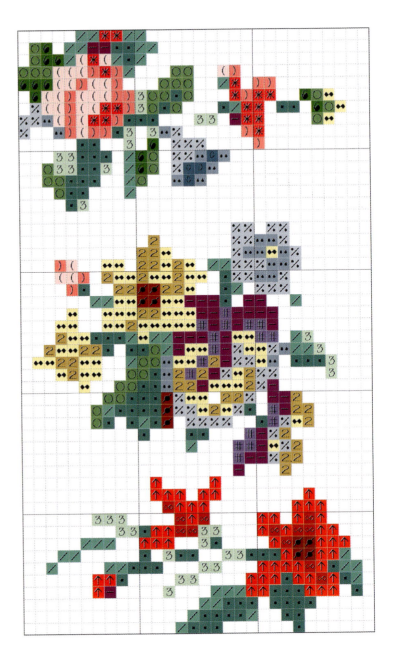

—	327	%	932
3	504	••	931
/	503	°	3750
•	501	(	3713
O	3347	)	760
ϐ	3345	✳	3328
••	744	↑	350
2	833	◇◇	355
ϕ	433	#	3746

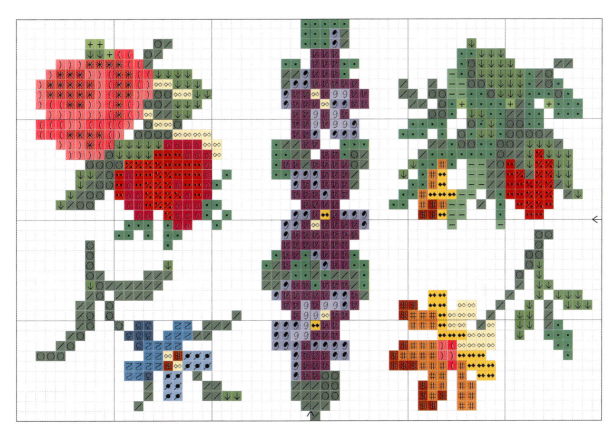

						—	368	◇◇	745
%	304	2	334	(	3354	)	3731	o	814
3	312	↑	3347	●	340	●	3755	••	816
O	319	+	3348	6	341	4	550	$	975
•	320	✳	3350	/	367	••	743	#	977

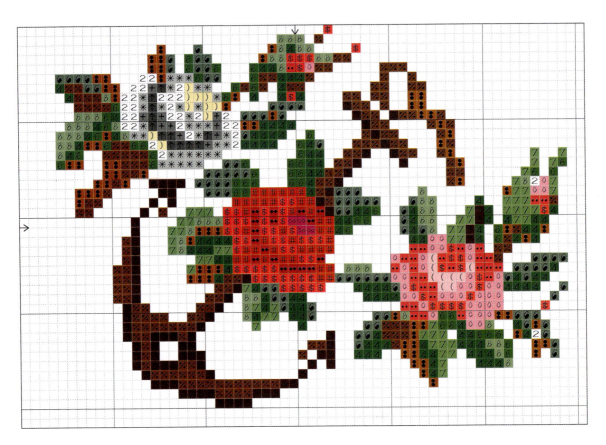

2	white	+	3787	◇◇	814
✳	3023	✞	433	◆◆	815
••	309	#	498	4	890
$	321	)	745	○	899
3	3371	(	776	6	986
✿	367	%	801	7	988
				8	989

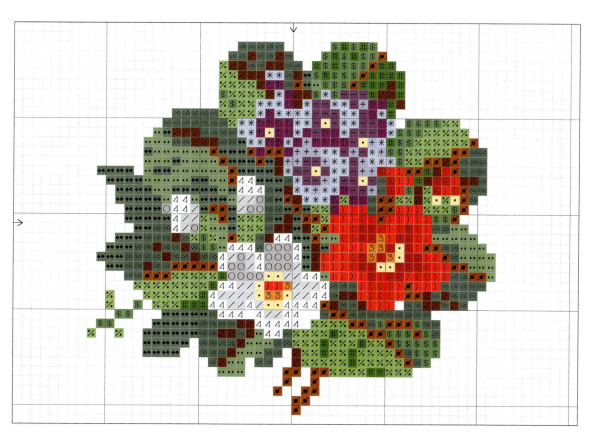

		#	3346		—	550
4	white	$	3347		O	648
(	304	%	3348		•	745
/	3072	+	341		∘	815
∞	319	◆◆	367		2	898
)	321	✳	3747		3	977
↑	327	♦	433		••	989

$ 3041

3042

* 3045

/ 319

O 367

o 3685

↑ 3687

• 3688

∞ 3740

◆◆ 3743

— 502

•• 676

(743

% 745

) 783

+ 869

◆ 987

2 988

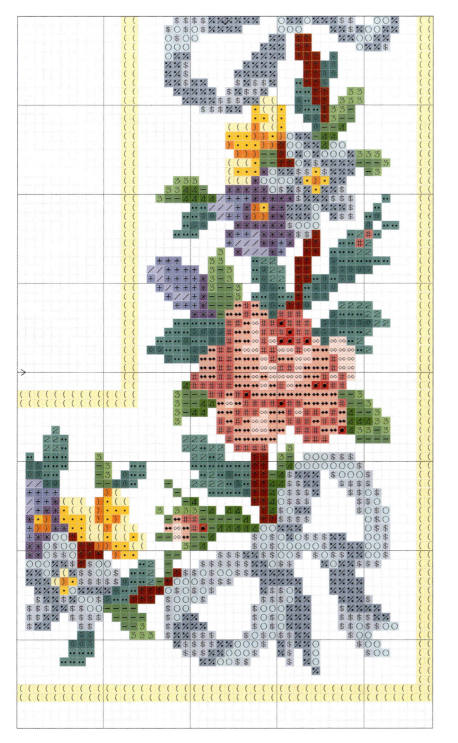

◇◇	225
◆◆	224
#	223
❡	3721
/	341
+	340
✳	3746
O	3752
$	932
%	931
3	3348
—	3347
4	3346
2	503
••	502
o	501
(	744
•	743
)	977
↑	433

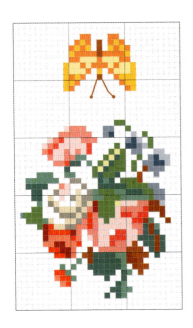

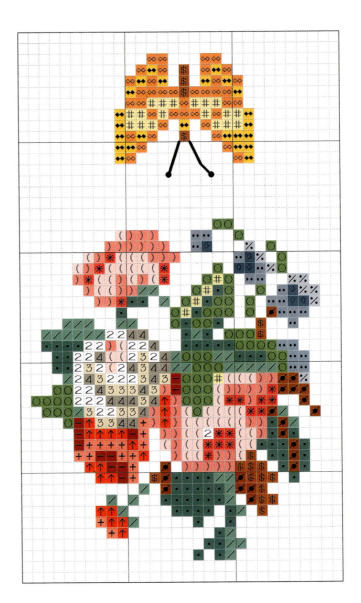

↑	350	∞	722
—	3777	#	744
•	501	◆◆	743
/	503	%	932
O	3347	••	931
$	435	o	3750
●	434	(	3713
2	blanc	)	760
3	3033	*	3328
4	3032	+	352

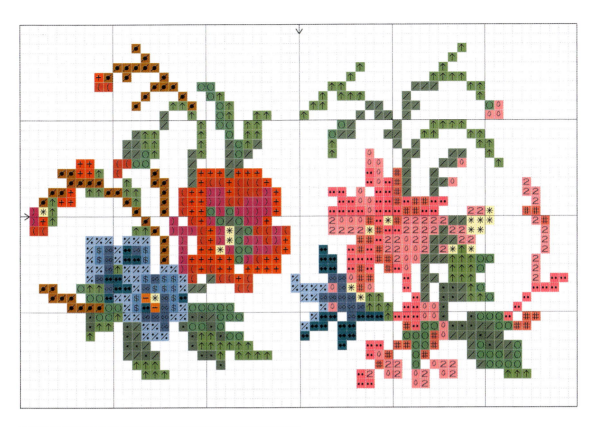

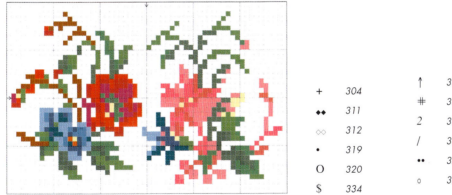

+	304	↑	3347	%	3755
◆◆	311	#	3350	◖	433
◇◇	312	2	3354	✳	744
•	319	/	367	)	814
O	320	••	3731	(	816
$	334	○	3733	—	922

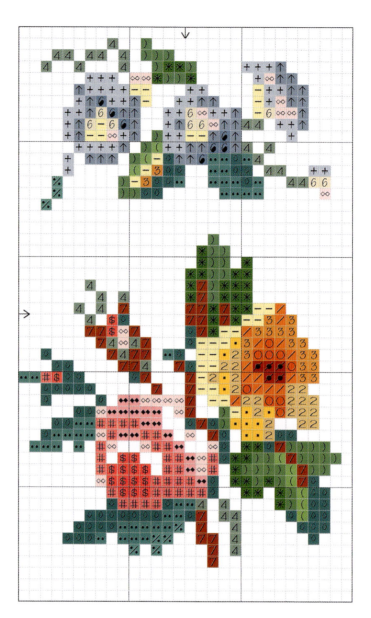

↑	931	◇◇	3713
●	930	◆◆	761
—	744	#	760
•	743	$	3712
2	676	%	503
3	729	••	502
6	3033	o	501
/	977	(	3348
O	976	)	3347
∮	975	*	3346
7	434	4	3053
		+	932

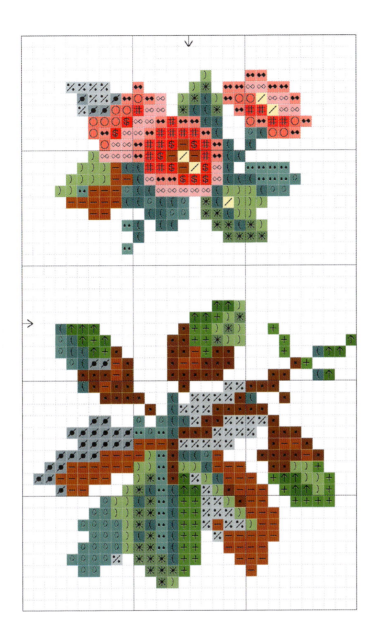

∞∞	761		
♦♦	760	(	501
O	3712	)	3348
#	3328	✳	3347
$	347	+	470
%	927	↑	469
⬢	926	—	434
••	503	•	801
○	502	/	744

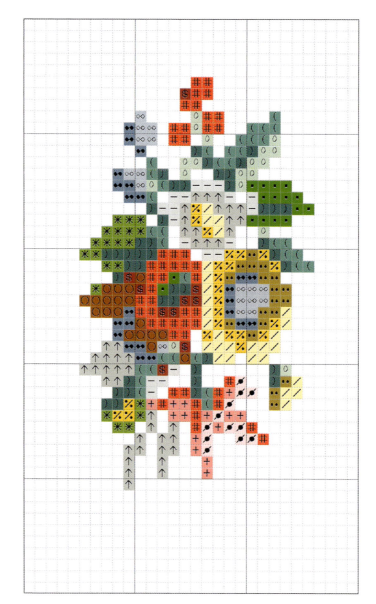

O	434	♠	3713
o	504	+	760
(	503	#	350
)	501	$	3777
✳	471	◇◇	932
•	470	◆◆	930
—	822	/	744
↑	644	%	743
		••	832

⬦⬦	932		
♦♦	931	—	504
$	744	3	503
%	743	•	502
••	3713	/	501
○	761	O	3347
(	760	⬗	3345
)	350	4	341
✳	355	⬗	340
+	834	#	3746
↑	434	2	327

○	304		
—	319	↑	744
$	320	••	816
(	350	◆◆	890
#	367	)	930
%	3777	✳	931
◇◇	725	+	932

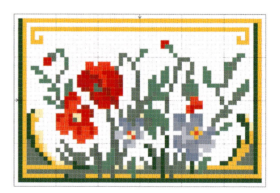

4	blanc	+	341		
(	304	◆◆	367	◦	815
◇◇	319	◖	3716	O	816
)	321	✳	3747	2	898
↑	327	7	433	◖	961
#	3346	—	550	3	977
$	3347	/	552	6	988
%	3348	•	745	••	989

A. Rouyer, n° 352

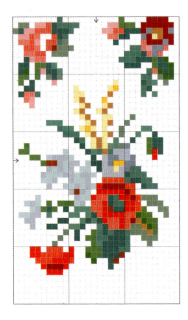

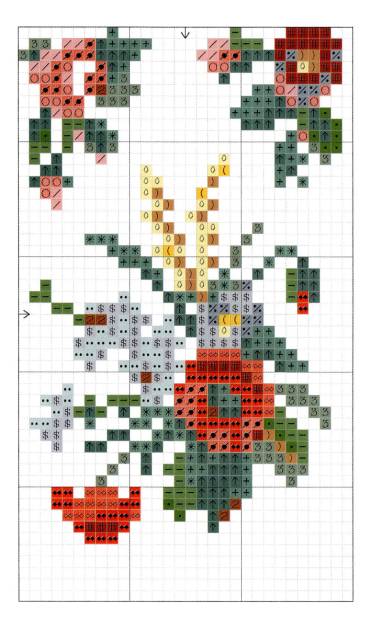

(	743
)	422
✳	503
+	502
↑	501
3	3053
—	3347
•	3346
2	434

/	761
O	760
❻	3712
◇◇	351
◆◆	350
#	3777
••	3752
$	932
%	931
o	744

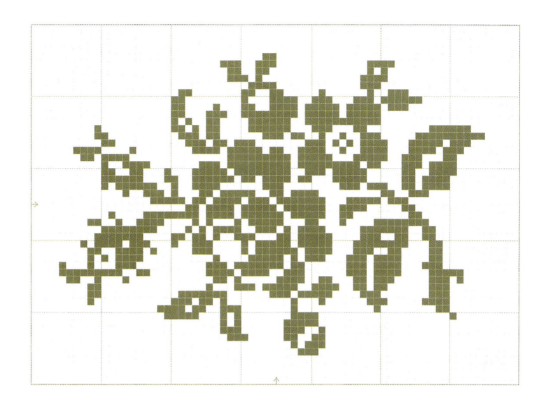

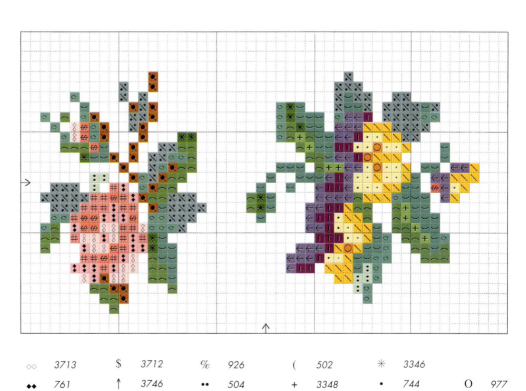

◇◇	3713	$	3712	%	926	(	502	✳	3346		
◆◆	761	↑	3746	••	504	+	3348	•	744	O	977
#	760	—	327	o	503	)	3347	/	743	♦	435

At the top: Godchaux design (Compell Frères collection); at the bottom: A. Rouyer, nº 177

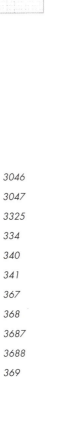

♦	3747	o		3046
4	3755	(		3047
✳	3803	/		3325
••	3828	•		334
☐	520	3		340
O	744	2		341
$	869	♥		367
◇◇	920	⌐		368
)	921	+		3687
—	963	↑		3688
		#		369

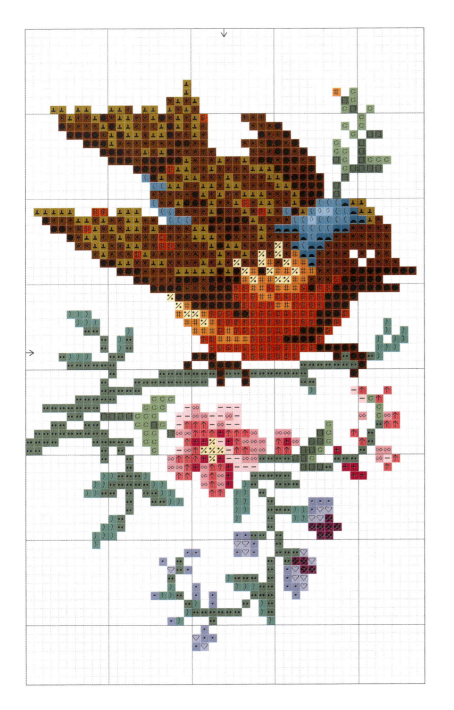

✳	327		○	519
•	340		%	745
♡	341		✳	801
••	367		⊥	831
↑	3687		$	920
∞	3688		●	938
(	3760		—	963
+	3803		#	977
)	502		□	987
⁃	517		c	989

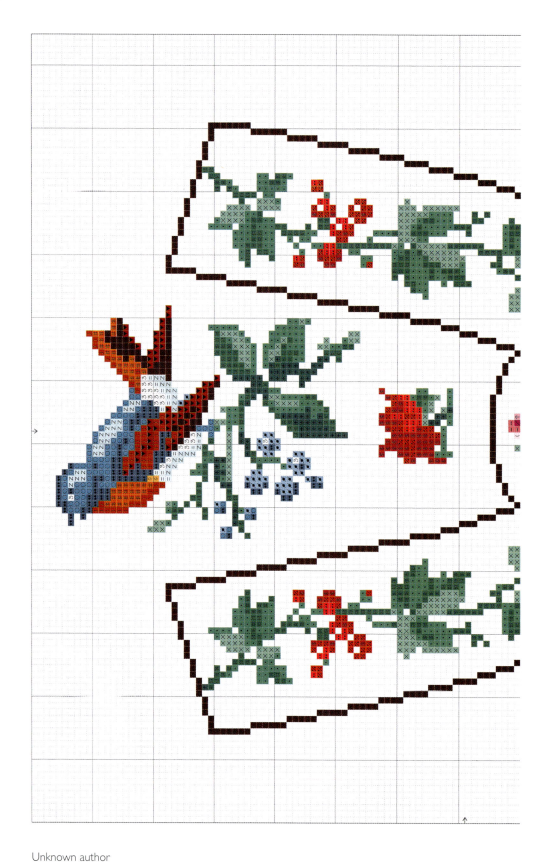

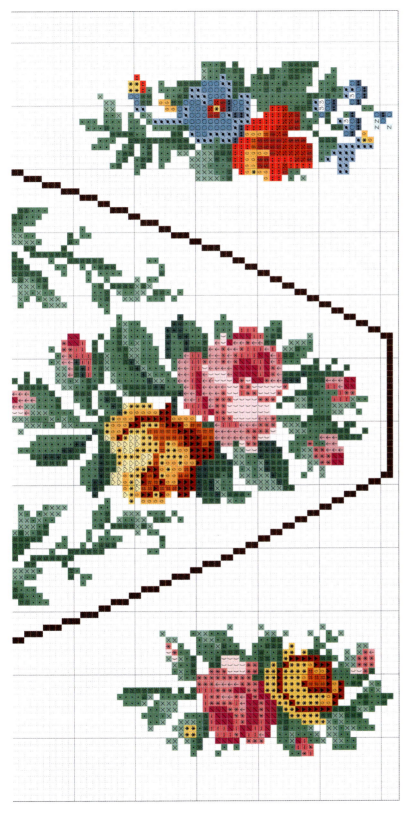

3	*white*
◆◆	*312*
••	*321*
O	*334*
✳	*3354*
◇◇	*3371*
/	*3685*
—	*3687*
↑	*3688*
❡	*3755*
=	*3756*
○	*3820*
†	*3822*
%	*498*
+	*500*
|||	*561*
•	*562*
×	*563*
♡	*745*
Z	*775*
$	*815*
(	*818*
▼	*918*
)	*920*
#	*922*
•	*977*

INDEX OF DESIGNS BY LETTER HEIGHT

STITCHES	ALBUM Nº	PAGE
5	Sajou, nº 1	23
	Sajou, nº 2	30
	Sajou, nº 3	40
	Alexandre, nº 211	22
7	Sajou, nº 2	25
	Sajou, nº 103	27
	Alexandre, nº 211	22
8	Sajou, nº 104	44
9	Sajou, nº 3	18
	Sajou, nº 7	41
	Alexandre, nº 98	45
	Alexandre, nº 211	22
10	Sajou, nº 2	29
	Sajou, nº 3	14
	Sajou, nº 3	17
	Sajou, nº 53	51
	Sajou, nº 103	34-36
	Sajou, nº 103	34-36
	Sajou, nº 103	34-36
	Alexandre, nº 98	46
11	Sajou, nº 3	13
	Sajou, nº 3	16
12	Sajou, nº 2	31
	Sajou, nº 3	15
13	Rouyer, nº 152	162
14	Sajou, nº 149	37
15	Sajou, nº 2	39
	Sajou, nº 7	19
	Rouyer	32
16	Sajou, nº 52	21
17	Sajou, nº 52	21
	Sajou, nº 204	59
19	Sajou, nº 184	232
20	Sajou, nº 182	342
	Sajou, nº 606	218

STITCHES	ALBUM N°	PAGE
21	Sajou, n°53	51
	Sajou, n° 605	61
23	Sajou, n° 182	264
	Sajou, n° 605	65
25	Sajou, n° 149	42
	Rouyer, n° 152	162
27	Alexandre, n° 144	47
28	Alexandre, n° 229	130
	Sajou, n° 164	300
	Sajou, n° 323	194
29	Sajou, n° 52	50
	Sajou, n° 322	160
	Sajou, n° 653	178
30	Sajou, n° 203	52, 96
	Sajou, n° 604	172
31	Sajou, n° 653	176
	Sajou, n° 656	84
32	Sajou, n° 204	54
	Sajou, n° 605	76
33	Sajou, n° 205	180, 184
	Sajou, n° 605	74
	Sajou, n° 606	186, 192
	Rouyer, n° 248	92, 146
	Rouyer, n° 249	111
	Alexandre, n° 211	104
	LV, n° 1	260
34	Sajou, n° 205	226
	Sajou, n° 604	167
35	Rouyer, n° 248	150
	Rouyer, n° 249	108
	Sajou, n° 184	234
	Sajou, n° 362	230
36	LV, n° 1	334
37	Sajou, n° 182	243
38	Rouyer, n° 145	336
40	Sajou, n° 322	206, 214
	Sajou, n° 325	210

STITCHES	ALBUM N°	PAGE
	Sajou, n° 656	88
41	Sajou, n° 323	204
	Sajou, n° 654	79
42	Rouyer, n° 293	320
43	Rouyer, n° 152	100
	Sajou, n° 182	338
45	Sajou, n° 184	344
	Sajou, n° 204	56
46	Sajou, n° 184	326
48	Alexandre, n° 211	116
53	Rouyer, n° 293	304
54	Sajou, n° 151	154
55	Rouyer, n° 144	329
	Rouyer, n° 293	310
56	Alexandre, n° 229	132, 138
	Rouyer, n° 292	306
57	Rouyer, n° 145	266
	Sajou, n° 325	198
59	Alexandre, n° 224	126
	Rouyer, n° 145	239
	Rouyer, n° 146	256
60	Alexandre, n° 224	146
	Rouyer, n° 144	322
66	Sajou, n° 606	186
67	Sajou, n° 604	167
	Sajou, n° 605	70
77	Sajou, n° 605	61
80	Sajou, n° 606	218
85	LV, n° 1	247
103	Sajou, n° 603	272

INDEX OF BORDERS BY SIZE

WIDTH/ HEIGHT	MOTIF	ALBUM N°	PAGE
126-170	Flowers	Sajou, n° 185	321
	Butterfly Corner	Sajou, n° 185	
125-171	Corner	Sajou, n° 186	322
126-171	Cups/teapot Corner	Sajou, n° 186	323
	Birds/hens	Sajou, n° 185	385
	Swans/dragons Borders	Sajou, n° 185	394
	Hens/flowers Checkerboard	Sajou, n° 186	397
	Floral corner motif Centered motif	Sajou, n° 185	399
	Flowers and flower basket	Sajou, n° 186	401
	Moon/anchor/horseshoe Borders	Sajou, n° 186	387
	Corners	Sajou, n° 185	389
	Dragons/borders	Sajou, n° 186	392
	Borders/checkerboard	Sajou, n° 185	393
	Floral borders Corner embroidery	Sajou, n° 185	390
130-90	Violet/flowers Art nouveau	Berlin	404
	Art nouveau flowers	Berlin	405
	Art nouveau flower Corner design	Berlin	406
	Flowers/borders	Berlin	407, 402

Acknowledgments

I would like to thank everyone who has offered me their help and designs, and in particular,
those friends who have helped me with their embroidery work:

Martine Bazin, Michèle Clément, Cécile Delatouche, Béatrice Delaume, Martine Duhamel, Mireille Gardet,
Maria-Alice Geoffroy, Josette Gougaut, Martine Labrousse, Evelyne Lavaud-Gras, Marie-José Lemercier, Sylvaine Lenoir,
Olivier Magadoux, Annie Plourde, Roselyne Pottier, Liliane Renollet, Christine Schmitt, Brigitte Souchier, Marie-Annick
Villedieu, Marie-Noëlle Vincent, as well as my daughters Céline, Emilie, Charlotte, Adélaïde,
and the whole team at Flammarion.